The Goodword
Book of
Quran
People
For # Kids

This book belongs to:

_____

First published 2005
Reprinted 2014
© Goodword Books 2014
Editor: Vinni Rahman

Goodword Books
1, Nizamuddin West Market, New Delhi-110 013
Tel. +9111-4182-7083, Mob. +91-8588822672
email: info@goodwordbooks.com
www.goodwordbooks.com

Islamic Vision Ltd.
434 Coventry Road, Small Heath
Birmingham B10 0UG, U.K.
Tel. 121-773-0137
Fax: 121-766-8577
e-mail: info@ipci-iv.co.uk
www.islamicvision.co.uk

Goodword Books, Chennai
324, Triplicane High Road
Triplicane, Chennai-600005
Tel. +9144-4352-4599
Mob. +91-9790853944, 9600105558
email: chennaigoodword@gmail.com

Printed in India

IB Publisher Inc.
81 Bloomingdale Rd, Hicksville
NY 11801, USA
Tel. 516-933-1000
Fax: 516-933-1200
Toll Free: 1-888-560-3222
email: info@ibpublisher.com
www.ibpublisher.com

The Goodword
Book of
Quran
People
For Kids

Saniyasnain Khan

GOODWORD

How to Use this Book

The Quran is a book of guidance. It tells us to worship Allah and do good works so that He may be pleased with us. Apart from that the Quran is full of exciting stories, adventures, teachings and prayers, which show Allah's love for us and explain what He requires from us as believers and as His sincere servants. This book deals mainly with the many people and nations mentioned in the Quran. Some of the people were great prophets. Some formed tribes or nations. Some were kings and queens. Some were good and pious, while others were wicked and sinful.

In telling the stories of these people, the aim of the Quran is to tell us how to live in this world. These stories thus act as warning to us, show us the right way and stop us from doing bad things.

This book contains biographies of almost all the people mentioned in the Quran. Every biography consists of 6-8 parts.

1. **Name**—It gives the name of the person or tribe.

2. **Biography**—Some biographies are short, and some are long. It depends on how much detail is given in the Quran about that person or group of persons. Each biography focuses on the message and lessons that we can receive from it. This is to help us to become good believers.

3. **Moral**—This is the main point of the story. It is what we must learn from the story and remember so as to become good believers.

4. **Key Events**—This gives a summary of the main events in the story.

5. **Reference in the Quran**—It helps the reader to go back to the Quran and read the relevant passage so as to know more about the story.

6. **Cross Reference in the Book**—This helps in referring to stories which are connected with each other.

7. **Relatives**—This gives more information about the relatives of the main character, so that the reader may have a good idea of the people connected with the story.

8. **Study Question**—This deals with the message of the story and how it is relevant to us today. It helps us to understand the message of the Quran in a better way.

That's it! *The Goodword Book of Quran People for Kids* isn't hard to use. It's just fun and packed with information. It's here for you any time you need to learn about the people of the Quran. We hope you like it.

May Allah help you study the message and wisdom of the Quran.

Abdullah ibn Ubayy

Abdullah ibn Ubayy was a leader of Madinah's hypocrites and pagans (*munafiqun*). He pretended to be with the Muslims but was never on their side. He had secretly hated the Prophet Muhammad since the time of the Hijrah. He dreamt of becoming the ruler of Madinah and saw the Prophet's growing popularity and strength as a threat. Therefore, he worked against him and the interests of the Muslims.

He plotted against the Muslims with various Quraysh leaders and Jewish tribes like the Banu Nadir. It was his treachery which was mainly responsible for the defeat of the Muslims at the battle of Uhud. At the last moment, he turned back from the battleground along with his 300 men. He also played a major role in spreading lies about the Prophet's wife, Aishah.

In spite of his treacherous acts, the Prophet did not allow his Companions to kill him. When he died, the Prophet himself led his burial prayer.

▶ **Moral**: Jealousy and wrong ambition lead to evil. Hypocrites should not be trusted.

▶ **Key Events**: Battle of Uhud, scandal against Aishah.

▶ **See the Quran:** *At-Tawba* 9:84; *An-Nur* 24:11-12 *Al-Munafiqun* 63:8.

▶ **See in this book:** Al-Munafiqun.

▶ **Study Question:** Why did Abdullah ibn Ubayy hate the Prophet Muhammad?

Abdullah ibn Umm Maktum

Abdullah ibn Umm Maktum, a blind man, was one of the early converts to Islam. He once came to the Prophet Muhammad to listen to the Quran while the Prophet was busy explaining it to the pagan Quraysh. The Prophet did not like his untimely arrival and spoke abruptly to him. Allah did not like this and *Surah* 80, *Abasa* (He Frowned), was revealed which expressed Allah's displeasure at the Prophet's attitude. Since then the Prophet always treated Abdullah ibn Umm Maktum with great respect. He even appointed him the Governor of Madinah.

▶ **Moral**: One should not be rude to anyone at any time because Allah does not like this. Rank and position do not make anyone superior to any other.

▶ **Key Events**: Revelation of *Surah* 80, *Abasa* (He Frowned).

▶ **See the Quran:** *Abasa* 80:1-12.

▶ **Study Question**: Why did Allah become unhappy with the Prophet?

Abraha

Abraha was the Ethiopian Christian King who ruled Yemen in 6 A.D. He decided to destroy the Ka'bah and set out for Makkah with an army of sixty thousand soldiers and a dozen elephants.The Makkans were helpless and unable to protect the House of Allah. At that time a flock

of birds flew over the army and showered small stones on it which they were carrying in their beaks. Later the soldiers were struck by small pox. Many of them, including King Abraha, died while returning to their country. This incident happened in 570 A.D., the year the Prophet Muhammad was born.

▶ **Moral**: One should never be arrogant about his position and power.

▶ **Key Events**: March towards Makkah to destroy the Ka'bah.

▶ **See the Quran**: *Al-Fil,* 105:1-5.

▶ **See in this book**: *Ashab al-Fil.*

▶ **Study Question**: How were the Makkans and the Ka'bah saved from the attack of King Abraha?

Abu Bakr

Abu Bakr was the closest and the most loyal companion of the Prophet Muhammad. He was a rich and powerful merchant of the Taym tribe in Makkah. He was a man of noble character and was full of kindness. He was the first important person to be get converted to Islam outside the family of the Prophet Muhammad. Abu Bakr brought younger men of Makkah into the religion. He freed many slaves, including Bilal ibn Rabah. Due to his faith in Islam he suffered financial losses and other cruelties at the hands of the Quraysh. He was insulted, abused and dust was thrown on him. Like other believers, even he was forced to pray in private.

He accompanied the Prophet on his Hijrah from Makkah to Madinah in 622 A.D. He was always with the Prophet in all important events. He also had his daughter, Aishah, married to the Prophet Muhammad.

In 632 A.D., when the Prophet Muhammad died, it was Abu Bakr who consoled the Muslims and held them together. He became the first Caliph, the chief representative of Islam. During his Caliphate, Iraq and Syria also accepted Islam. He played a major role in the spread of the message of the Quran. In 634 A.D., he died and was buried in the Prophet's mosque at Madinah.

Due to his unshakeable faith, he held the title of 'Siddiq' – one who testifies to the truth.

▶ **Moral:** His life is an example of a perfect follower of Islam. It highlights the qualities of faith and loyalty.

▶ **Key events**: Conversion to Islam, Hijrah with the Prophet Muhammad, the Prophet Muhammad's death, his becoming the first Caliph.

▶ **See the Quran:** *At-Tawba,* 9:40.

▶ **See in this book:** Aishah, Ali ibn Abu Talib, Al-Ansar, Al-Muhajirun, Muhammad, Sahaba, Umar ibn Al-Khattab, and Uthman ibn Affan.

▶ **Relatives**: Son-in-law – the Prophet Muhammad

Daughter – Aishah, Asma

Son – Abd al-Ka'bah

Wife – Umm Ruman

▶ **Study Question**: Say how Abu Bakr was the closest and the most loyal companion of the Prophet Muhammad.

Abu Jahal

Abu Jahal was one of the chiefs of the Quraysh. He was strongly against the Prophet. He was the leader of those who opposed the Prophet Muhammad. His actual name was Abu al-Hakam, but the Muslims renamed him 'Abu Jahal', the father of ignorance. He was jealous of the Prophet and was deeply disturbed by his religious message. He harassed the Prophet and his followers and did not even let them pray in front of the Ka'bah. Along with Abu Lahab and Abu Sufiyan he planned to kill the Prophet before the Hijrah.

He also led an army of more than a thousand strong against the Muslims in the battle of Badr. Though the Muslims and many of the Quraysh also were not inclined to do battle, it was Abu Jahal who insisted on it. He died in this battle.

▶ **Moral**: People who deny the truth and create obstacles to the acceptance of truth are ignorant and foolish. They will surely be cast into hell.

▶ **Key Events**: Hijra, Battle of Badr.

▶ **See the Quran**: *Al-Alaq,* 96:9-16.

▶ **See in this book:** Muhammad.

▶ **Relatives:**   Son   –   Ikrimah

▶ **Study Question:** What did Abu Jahal do against the Prophet Muhammad and his followers?

Why was he called Abu Jahal?

Abu Lahab

Abu Lahab was an uncle of the Prophet Muhammad. He and his wife, Arwa, were most vicious and violent enemies of the Prophet. They carried on a non-stop campaign against him. They humiliated and troubled him and killed his followers. Abu Lahab was also a part of the group of enemies of the Prophet who plotted to stop the spread of Islam and even to kill him.

After the death of Abu Talib, Abu Lahab became the chief of his tribe, Banu Hashim. This not only increased the Prophet's troubles but also put his life in danger. Abu Lahab died soon after the battle of Badr.

The Quran describes Abu Lahab as the 'father of flame' due to his violent nature. Allah gave the assurance that neither his position as chief of his tribe nor his wealth would save him from the fire of hell.

▶ **Moral**: Allah's justice will surely be done. All of us have to be responsible for our acts and beliefs.

▶ **Key Events**: The Prophet's Hijrah, the message of Islam.

▶ **See the Quran:** *Surah Al-Lahab* or *Surah Al-Masad,* 111:1-5.

▶ **See in this book:** Arwa.

▶ **Relatives**:

Nephew   -   The Prophet Muhammad

Wife   -   Arwa

▶ **Study Question**: Why is Abu Lahab described as the 'father of flame'?

The Ad

The Ad were believers in the Prophet Nuh (Noah). They lived in ancient Yemen. They were descendants of Iram, one of the grandsons of the Prophet Nuh. They later came to be known as the Ad people. In the beginning, they followed the path of Allah. But, as they became rich and prosperous, they also became proud and left the path of Allah. They began to worship statues—Sada, Samuda and Hara.

The Prophet Hud was sent to them. He asked them to worship Allah, the one and only God, and not their false statues. He also asked them to be humble and not to be cruel to the weak. They did not listen

to him. Instead they even made fun of him. There was a famine for three years, but they still refused to listen to him. Finally, a terrible rainstorm destroyed everyone except those who believed in Allah and followed the message of Prophet Hud.

▶ **Moral**: When material prosperity makes people proud, they leave the path of Allah and thereby bring on their own destruction.

▶ **Key Events**: Material development, becoming proud, leaving the path of Allah, their destruction.

▶ **See the Quran**: *Al-Araf* 7:65-72; *Hud* 11:50-60; *Al-Furqan* 25:38; *Ash-Shuaraa* 26:123-140; *Al-Ankabut* 29:38; *Fussilat* 41:15-16; *Al-Ahqaf* 46:21-26,128; *Az-Zariyat* 51:41-42; *Al-Qamar* 54:18-21; *Al-Haqqah* 69:4-8; *Al-Fajr* 89:6-14.

▶ **See in this book**: Hud.

▶ **Study Question**: Who were the Ad?

Why did they start worshipping statues?

What was the Prophet Hud's message to the Ad?

Adam

Adam was the first man created by Allah. He was also the first prophet. He is honoured by the title of Abu'l-Bashr (The Father of Mankind). Allah also created the first woman, Hawwa (Eve), as the wife and loving companion of Adam. Allah made Adam from dry clay. After giving him a human form, Allah breathed His spirit into him. Unlike the angels who were only pure and devout, Allah gave him emotions such as love and understanding. He also gave Adam knowledge and the intelligence to choose between right and wrong. All these faculties, which raised him above the angels, could also make him do evil, which by training of his will, he had to learn to reject. These faculties could lead him to the highest good, but also drag him to the lowest evil.

Then Allah asked the angels to bow before Adam. All of them did so except the proud Iblis (Satan). He did not obey Allah because he believed that he was superior to Adam as he was made of fire. Allah asked him to go away and deprived him of His Grace. Later, due to Iblis' prayers, Allah granted him respite till the Day of Judgement.

One day Iblis whispered evil to Adam and Hawwa, who lived in the Gardens of Paradise in a state of innocence and complete peace.

He made them believe that he was their real friend and well-wisher. At his suggestion, they ate a fruit from the forbidden tree which Allah had instructed them not even to go near. But Iblis told them that eating the fruit from this tree would make them angels and they would live forever. Till then they did not know evil but, with their disobedience, they committed a sin and thus brought about their own downfall. He begged for Allah's forgiveness. Allah is merciful. He pardoned them but asked them to go down on earth. He warned them that Iblis was going to be their enemy till the Day of Judgement and would tempt mankind into evil by making what was unfair look fair to them.

Allah said that from time to time His prophets would come to guide mankind to the right path. Only those human beings would be saved from Iblis who followed Allah's guidance and the rest would go to hell.

▶ **Moral**: Life on earth is temporary and a test for mankind. Man should use his faculties of emotions, love, knowledge and intelligence to make choices and decisions in accordance with Allah's will. Iblis cannot harm the true worshippers of Allah.

▶ **Key Events**: Creation of Adam, Iblis' disobedience, Adam's disobedience and Allah's forgiveness.

▶ **See the Quran**: *Al-Baqarah* 2:30-39; *Al-Araf* 7:19-25,112; *Al-Hijr* 15:26, 29; *Ta-Ha* 20:120-121; *As-Sajdah* 32:9; *Sad* 38:72-85.

▶ **See in this book:** Habil and Qabil.

▶ **Relatives**: Wife - Hawwa

 Son - Habil

 Qabil

▶ **Study Question**: Why is the human being Allah's superior creation?

Why did Iblis refuse to bow in front of Adam?

What brought about Adam's fall?

How can human beings save themselves from Iblis?

Al-Ahbar

Al-Ahbar is the term used for ancient Jewish scholars and priests. They are generally denounced for the various sins committed by them. They spread lies, ate forbidden things, fooled people out of their money and possessions and stopped people from following the correct path of Allah.

▶ **Moral**: Piety and goodness are not necessarily the virtues of priests and scholars. Excess of power can take people away from the path of Allah.

▶ **See the Quran**: *Al-Maidah* 5:63; *At-Tawba* 9:34.

▶ **See in this book**: Ahl al-kitab and Ar-Ruhban.

▶ **Study Question**: What sort of people were Al-Ahbar?

What happens when people gain an excess of power?

Ahl al-Bayt

Ahl al-Bayt means the People of the House. This term is used in the Quran for the wives of the Prophet Muhammad. In general it is used for the whole family of the Prophet, including descendants through his daughter, Fatimah, and his cousin and son-in-law, Ali ibn Abu Talib,—who had three sons—Hasan, Husain and Muhsin (Muhsin died in infancy). Even those who took part in the mission of the Prophet were part of Ahl al-Bayt.

▶ **Moral**: It is not only the blood relations that make a family but even the followers of the same belief are like a family.

▶ **Key Events**: The Prophet Muhammad's life, the coming of Islam.

▶ **See the Quran:** *Al-Ahzab* 33:33.

▶ **See in this book:** Aishah, Ali ibn Abu Talib, Khadijah, the Prophet Muhammad and Ummahat al-Muminin.

▶ **Study Question**: What do you understand by Ahl al-Bayt?

Ahl al-Injil

Ahl al-Injil is the phrase used for the People of the Gospel. The Quran has the same message of Allah that was recorded in earlier books, before it was corrupted by their followers. The words of Allah in the Torah and the Injil are preserved in the Quran. Therefore, they should be believed in.

▶ **Moral**: Pride makes one forget even one's own beliefs.

▶ **Key Events**: The coming of Islam.

▶ **See the Quran**: *Al-Maidah* 5:47.

▶ **See in this book**: Ahl al-Kitab and An-Nasara.

▶ **Study Question**: What do you understand by Ahl al-Injil?

Ahl al-Kitab

Ahl al-Kitab means the People of the Book. They are the people who were given the divine scriptures (books) before the Quran. In general, the Quran gives them a special place. There are some upright people among them who believe in Allah and the Day of Judgement and do only what is right. The Quran asks the Muslims to argue with them courteously and encourages discussions on mutually held beliefs.

The Quran condemns the ancient People of the Book for two main sins—rejection of the last Prophet (Muhammad) and treating their priests as lords, which is an insult to Allah. It also talks about their other sins, like killing of the prophets, moving away from the path of Allah and making changes (*tahrif*) in the divine scriptures to suit their own interests. The Muslims are allowed to eat the food (*dhabiha*) of the People of the Book, and are also allowed to marry their womenfolk but not their men.

▶ **Moral**: Pride and power turn people into sinners. The People of the Book even refused to believe that the Prophet Muhammad was the last Prophet as mentioned in their scriptures and, therefore, fell into sin.

▶ **Key Events**: The coming of Islam.

▶ **See the Quran:** *Al-Baqarah* 2:75, 91,146; *Aal Imran* 3:64, 81,110,113,114; *An- Nisaa* 4:46; *Al-Maidah* 5:5,13,41; *At-Tawba* 9:31; *Al-Ankabut* 29:46; *Al-Hadid* 57:28.

▶ **See in this book:** Ahl al Injil, Banu Israil and An-Nasara.

▶ **Study Question**: What are the sins committed by the Ahl al-Kitab?

Why does the Quran give a special place to the Ahl al-Kitab?

Ahl Yathrib

Ahl Yathrib means the People of Madinah. The Quran also calls them Ahl al-Madinah. Yathrib was the ancient name of Madinah. After the Hijrah of the Prophet Muhammad, it came to be known as Madinat an-Nabi, or Al-Madinah. The population of Madinah belonged mainly to two tribes—Al-Aws and Al-Khazraj. They had continuously been fighting with each other for about 40 years. Their enmity ended with the Prophet Muhammad's message of peace. The Muslim members of these tribes were called Al-Ansar. They played an important role in the history of Islam.

▶ **Moral**: Beliefs can unite even enemies in brotherhood.

▶ **Key Events**: Hijrah of the Prophet Muhammad.

▶ **See the Quran:** *Al-Imran* 3:103; *At-Tawba* 9:101; *Al-Ahzab* 33:13.

▶ **See in this book:** Al-Ansar.

▶ **Study Question**: How did the enmity between the two tribes end?

Aishah

The Prophet Muhammad married Aishah after the death of his first wife, Khadijah. She was the daughter of Abu Bakr, one of the Prophet's closest companions. She was very intelligent and had an excellent memory. Most of the revelations to the Prophet in Madinah were made while she was with him.

She was a good companion and a devoted wife. Even after the Prophet's death she continued to be a great source of strength and inspiration to the Muslims. After his death she was an important authority on his life and religious practice. She narrated 2210 sayings and anecdotes of the Prophet, and these form the bedrock of traditional Islam. She holds an important place in the political and religious history of Islam.

Abdullah ibn Ubayy spread many lies about her. But she faced them with strength of character and determination. At that time *Surah* 24 *An-Nur* was revealed, which completely cleared her of the false charges and proved her innocence.

She had no children and died at the age of 66. She was buried in Al-Baqi in Madinah.

▶ **Moral**: In a marriage a wife and a husband are equal partners. A good and intelligent wife can continue the good works of her husband even after his death.

▶ **Key Events**: Marriage to the Prophet Muhammad.

▶ **See the Quran**: *An-Nur* 24:12.

▶ **See in this book**: Abu Bakr, Ahl al-Bayt, Muhammad and Ummahat al-Mu'minin.

▶ **Relatives**:   Husband   -   The Prophet Muhammad

Father   -   Abu Bakr

▶ **Study Question**: What sort of a person was Aishah?

What is the contribution of Aishah to the growth of Islam?

Aal Dawud

Aal Dawud is the term used in the Quran for the family of the Prophet Dawud (David).

▶ **Key Events**: Killing of Jalut, becoming king, the Prophet Dawud's message.

▶ **See in this book:** Dawud and Sulayman.

Aal Firawn

Aal Firawn means the people of Firawn (Pharaoh). The Quran uses this term to refer to the followers of Firawn.

▶ **Moral**: Everyone is responsible for his acts. One cannot blame the leader or the head of the family for one's sins.

▶ **Key Events:** Firawn's cruelties, birth of Prophet Musa (Moses), message of Prophet Musa.

▶ **See in this book:** Firawn, Musa, Qarun and Haman.

Aal Ibrahim

Aal Ibrahim is the term used in the Quran for the descendants of the Prophet Ibrahim (Abraham). The heirs of the Prophet Ibrahim received the scriptures. His heirs included over a dozen great prophets and some well-known kings. Prophet Muhammad too was a direct descendant of the Prophet Ibrahim.

▶ **Moral:** Some families are blessed. They are rewarded for their deeds by good and great descendants.

▶ **Key Events:** Message of the Prophet Ibrahim, birth of other prophets in his family and their messages.

▶ **See the Quran:** *An-Nisaa,* 4:54.

▶ **See in this book:** Hajar, Ibrahim, Ishaq, Ismail and Sarah.

▶ **Study Question:** What do you know about the descendants of the Prophet Ibrahim?

Aal Imran

Aal Imran (Amran) is the term given in the Quran for the family of Imran.

▶ **Moral:** This family was blessed with the birth of many prophets.

▶ **Key Events:** Life of the prophets born in this family.

▶ **See the Quran:** *Aal-Imran* 3.

▶ **See in this book:** Hannah, Harun, Imran, Maryam and Musa.

Aal Lut

Aal Lut is the term used for the family and followers of the Prophet Lut (Lot). Except for his wife, all of them were saved from the showers of fire and stones which fell on the inhabitants of the sinful cities, Sodom and Gomorrah, for their unspeakable crimes.

▶ **Moral:** Everyone is responsible for his or her own deeds. Even the family members of the messengers of Allah were also to be punished if they were sinners.

▶ **Key Events**: Message of the Prophet Lut, destruction of the sinners.

▶ **See in this book:** Lut and wife of Lut.

▶ **Study Question**: What happened to the cities of Sodom and Gomorrah?

Aal Musa

Aal Musa is the family of the Prophet Musa (Moses), as mentioned in the Quran.

▶ **Moral**: A true family is one which works together for the cause of Allah.

▶ **Key Events**: Birth of the Prophet Musa, his message.

▶ **See in this book**: Harun, Musa and Umm Musa.

Aal Yaqub

Aal Yaqub is the term used for the family of Prophet Yaqub (Jacob) in the Quran.

▶ **Key Events**: Life of the Prophet Yusuf (Joseph), final union of the family.

▶ **See in this book**: Al-Asbat, Binyamin, Yahuda, Yaqub and Yusuf.

Ali ibn Abu Talib

Ali was the first cousin of the Prophet Muhammad and was the second person to convert to Islam, the first being the Prophet's wife, Khadijah. When the Prophet Muhammad invited his clan to accept Islam, it was only the 13 year old Ali who believed in him. Throughout his life he remained one of the most faithful followers of the Prophet. He remained under the care of the Prophet after the death of his father, Abu Talib.

The Prophet was very fond of his young cousin. When the Prophet undertook the Hijrah with Abu Bakr, it was Ali who stayed behind wearing the Prophet's clothes in his bed so that the Quraysh, who

were planning to kill the Prophet, would not realise that he had already left Makkah.

Soon after winning the battle of Badr, the Prophet Muhammad gave his youngest daughter, Fatimah, to Ali in marriage. They had three sons—Hasan, Husain and Muhsin. Muhsin died in his infancy.

Ali was famous for his bravery and deep knowledge of Islamic law. He became the fourth Caliph of Islam in 656 AD. He believed that a Muslim ruler must not be cruel and should consider himself equal to his subjects. He felt that a ruler should share the problems of his subjects and also take their advice.

Ali was assassinated in a rebellion in 661 AD. His shrine is in Najaf in Iraq. His sermons, sayings and letters have been collected in the form of a book—*Nahajal-Balagha* (The Way of Eloquence).

▶ **Moral**: He was a faithful follower of Islam. A ruler should fear Allah and treat everyone equally.

▶ **Key Events**: Conversion to Islam, Hijrah, marriage to Fatimah, becoming the fourth Caliph, his death.

▶ **See the Quran**: *Ash-Shuaraa* 26:214.

▶ **See in this book**: Abu Bakr, Ahl al-Bayt, the Prophet Muhammad, Sahaba, Umar ibn Al-Khattab and Uthman ibn Affan.

▶ **Relatives**:

Cousin and father-in-law	-	The Prophet Muhammad
Father	-	Abu Talib
Wife	-	Fatimah
Sons	-	Hasan
	-	Husain
	-	Muhsin

▶ **Study Question**: How do we know that Ali was completely devoted to the Prophet Muhammad?

What are the qualities of a good Muslim ruler?

Alyasa

In the Quran the Prophet Alyasa (Elisha) is mentioned in the group of prophets who were 'favoured above the nations'. He was the disciple of the Prophet Ilyas (Elias, also known as Elijah). He lived in the northern kingdom of Israel in the ninth century B.C., during the troubled times of the kings of Judah and Israel.

The Prophet Alyasa had to combat many misfortunes, but he always remained on the path of Allah. He called upon his people to stop worshipping Baal, the sun god, and to worship Allah instead. He performed many miracles, such as curing leprosy, so as to make people believe in his message. Every prophet came with special gifts from

33

Allah to guide people to the correct path. They used the language and means which were understood by the people of those times. Some used miracles to show the signs of Allah; these were not uncommon at that time.

▶ **Moral**: The prophet never flinches from the path of Allah, even when in dire straits.

▶ **Key Events**: Worship of Baal, message of the Prophet Alyasa, miracles.

▶ **See the Quran**: *Al-An'am* 6:86; *Sad* 38:48.

▶ **See in this book:** Baal and Ilyas.

▶ **Study Question**: Why did the Prophet Alyasa perform miracles?

Ammar ibn Yasir

Ammar ibn Yasir was the first Makkan Muslim to have built a mosque in his home. It is believed that it is he who is referred to in *Surah Az-Zumar* 39:9 of the Quran.

His parents, Yasir and Sumaiya, were continually punished by the Quraysh for their belief in Allah. Ammar ibn Yasir was strong-willed and, even after seeing the painful fate which his parents suffered, did not distance himself from the faith.

In the early days of Islam, passing through the streets of Makkah the Prophet Muhammad once saw Ammar ibn Yasir and his family

being subjected to violence by the Quraysh. When he saw the Prophet, he asked him whether this was all he would get in this world. The Prophet told him to be patient and said he would surely be rewarded and would go to heaven.

▶ **Moral**: True faith is never shaken, even in the worst of sufferings. The faithful will surely be rewarded with a place in heaven.

▶ **Key Events**: Sufferings due to faith, making of the first mosque in Makkah.

▶ **See the Quran:** *Surah Az-Zumar* 39:9.

▶ **Relatives**:   Father   -   Yasir

                              Mother   -   Sumaiya

▶ **Study Question**: Why were Ammar ibn Yasir and his family continually punished by the Quraysh?

Al-Ansar

Al-Ansar means the helpers. This term is used for the early Muslims of Madinah. They helped the Prophet Muhammad and the *Muhajirs* (the migrants) after they went on the Hijrah (migration) from Makkah to Madinah, having faced persecution and suffered cruelty at the hands of the Quraysh.

Al-Ansar gave all possible moral and material assistance to the *Muhajirs*. Peace and belief in Allah fostered such a strong sense of brotherhood among them that the *Ansars* were always ready to forego their own rights for them. They felt privileged in helping the *Muhajirs*. The Quran makes special mention of them along with the *Muhajirs* as having earned Allah's blessings.

▶ **Moral**: No tie can be stronger than one based on faith and belief in Allah.

▶ **Key Events**: Hijrah.

▶ **See the Quran**: *Al-Anfal* 8:72; *At Tawba* 9:100; *Al-Hashr* 59:9; *Al-Munafiqun* 63:7.

▶ **See in this book**: Al-Muhajirun, Muhammad and Sahaba.

▶ **Study Question**: How did *al-Ansar* help the *Muhajirs*?

What was the source of brotherhood among the *Ansars* and *Muhajirs*?

Al-A'raab

Al-A'raab is the term used for the Bedouins, the desert Arabs of the Prophet Muhammad's times. They were mainly those who were living in and around Madinah. When Islam came to Madinah, several Bedouin tribes embraced it without really understanding or believing it. Among them there were some who were true believers, but some were weak in their faith. There were some who were non-believers too.

The Quran says that in the eyes of Allah true *iman* (faith) comes when one discovers it as a reality and it touches one's whole being. It is then that one is ready to make every kind of sacrifice for its cause.

▶ **Moral:** You do not become a believer only by just saying that you are a believer. Your whole being has to practice it with complete understanding and faith.

▶ **Key Events:** Hijrah.

▶ **See the Quran:** *At-Tawba* 9:97, 99,101; *Al-Hujurat* 49:14.

▶ **Study Question**: Who were the Al-A'raab?

Who is a true believer?

Arwa

Arwa was the wife of Abu Lahab and an aunt of the Prophet Muhammad. Like her husband she was a deadly enemy of the Prophet. She hated the Prophet so much that during the night she would tie bundles of thorns with ropes of twisted palm-leaf fibre and throw them in the Prophet's path in order to hurt him. The Quran says that, like her husband, she would not escape the fire of hell. She was the sister of Abu Sufyan and the aunt of Muawiya. Her full name was Arwa umm Jamil bint Harb ibn Umayya.

▶ **Moral**: Evil prepares its own fate. Wrong deeds eventually hurt their doer the most.

▶ **Key Events**: The Prophet Muhammad's teachings of Islam.

▶ **See the Quran**: *Al-Lahab* or *Al-Masad* 111:4-5.

▶ **See in this book:** Abu Lahab.

▶ **Relatives**:

Husband	-	Abu Lahab
Brother	-	Abu Sufiyan
Nephew	-	Muawiya

▶ **Study Question**: Who was Arwa?

What did Arwa do to hurt the Prophet Muhammad?

Al-Asbat

Al-Asbat is the term used for the twelve tribes who were the descendants of the Prophet Yaqub (Jacob). These tribes bore the names of his twelve sons. They were Rubil, Shamun, Yahuda, Isakhir, Yusuf, Misha, Binyamin, Hadd, Ashir, Dan, Naftali and Zabulun.

When the Prophet Musa (Moses) led the Children of Israel into the deserts of Sinai, their need for water became acute and there was none in sight. Allah then asked the Prophet Musa to hit a rock with his staff, whereupon twelve springs immediately gushed out. There was one spring for each tribe. It is said that this took place near Hareb, close to Mount Sinai.

▶ **Moral**: Allah takes care of his followers.

▶ **Key Events**: The Prophet Musa's striking of the rock.

▶ **See the Quran**: *Al-Baqarah* 2:60,136, 146; *Aal-Imran* 3:84; *An-Nisaa* 4:163; *Al-Araf* 7:160.

▶ **See in this book:** Children of Israel, Musa, Yaqub and Yusuf.

▶ **Study Question**: Who were the Al-Asbat?

What happened when the Prophet Musa led the Children of Israel into the deserts of Sinai?

Ashab Al-Fil

Ashab Al-Fil means the People of the Elephant. This term is used in the Quran for the army of Abraha, the Ethiopian Christian king who came to conquer Makkah in 570 A.D. His army included a dozen elephants, hence this name.

▶ **Moral**: Fools are never aware of the reality.

▶ **Key Events**: March towards Makkah.

▶ **See the Quran**: *Al-Fil* 105:1.

▶ **See in this book:** Abraha.

▶ **Study Question**: Who were the Ashab Al-Fil?

Who was Abraha?

Ashab Al-Ayka

Ashab Al-Ayka means the People of the Wood. Al-Ayka was a town or a large stretch of forest land. It seems that the People of the Wood is the other name of the People of Madyan (Ashab Madyan) or a group of people living in their neighbourhood. The Prophet Shuayb was sent to them. They were wrongdoers and were, therefore, destroyed by Allah.

▶ **Moral**: Every wrongdoer is punished.

▶ **Key Events**: The coming of the Prophet Shuayb, the destruction of the People of the Wood.

▶ **See in this book**: Ashab Madyan, Ashab ar-Rass and Shuayb.

▶ **Study Question**: Who were the Ashab Al-Ayka?

Ashab Al-Hijr

Ashab Al-Hijr means the People of the Rocky Land. There is a rocky tract called Jabal Hijr, about 150 miles north of Madinah, south of the Oasis of Tayma. This was the country of the Thamud. They were wrongdoers who rejected the teachings of the messengers. The Prophet Salih was sent to them.

▶ **Moral**: Pride leads to sin and destroys even the most powerful.

▶ **Key Events**: The coming of the Prophet Salih, destruction of the Ashab Al-Hijr.

▶ **See the Quran**: *Al-Hijr* 15:80.

▶ **See in this book**: Salih and Thamud.

▶ **Study Question**: Who were the Ashab Al-Hijr?

Ashab Al-Kahf

Ashab Al-Kahf means the People of the Cave. According to the Quran they were wonders among the signs of Allah.

This story is about the seven young men of Ephesus, an ancient city near the western coast of Turkey. It happened during the reign (249 to 251 A.D.) of the Roman king, Daqyanus (Decius). He was an idol worshipper and disliked the teachings of the Prophet Isa (Jesus) who asked people to worship one God. Daqyanus was cruel to all believers and even killed them.

The seven young men, who were of noble families, believed in the teachings of the Prophet Isa. When Daqyanus got to know about them he decided to kill them.To save their lives they hid in a cave. They trusted Allah and prayed for His protection.Their prayers were heard. Allah made them fall asleep. They woke up after more than 300 years. A dog, Qitmir, was also with them. When they woke up, the world had changed, the ruler was Theodosius II (408-450 A.D.) who was a believer, a Christian, like them and so were most of his subjects. When the king heard their story, he came to pay his respects to them and sought their blessings. When these young men died, a place of worship was built at their cave as a memorial. The ruins of that cave still exist.

▶   **Moral**: Allah helps those who trust in Him completely. Allah is all-powerful and everything, even time, works in accordance with Allah's will. There is surely life after death. Nothing remains forever, everything changes.

- ▶ **Key Events**: The long sleep and the waking up of the seven sleepers.

- ▶ **See the Quran**: *Al-Kahf* 18:9-31.

- ▶ **Study Question**: What do you learn from the story of the seven young men of Ephesus?

Ashab Musa

Ashab Musa is the term used for the companions of the Prophet Musa (Moses).

- ▶ **Key Events**: The message of the Prophet Musa.

- ▶ **See in this book:** Musa.

Ashab Al-Qarya

Ashab Al-Qarya means the People of the Village. This village is believed to be Antakya (Antioch) in Turkey, the former capital of Syria under the Romans. Three messengers—Sadiq, Saduq and Shalum were sent to them. But the people of the village did not listen to them and asked them to go away. They even stoned to death a man, who answered the call of the Prophet. Allah was pleased with him and called him one of the righteous.

▶ **Moral**: Sinners will never listen to the call of Allah.

▶ **Key Events**: The coming of the three messengers.

▶ **See the Quran**: *Yasin* 36:26, 27.

▶ **Study Question**: Who were the messengers sent to Antakya and what happened there?

Why did the Ashab Al-Qarya kill a man by stoning?

Ashab ar-Rass

Ashab ar-Rass means the People of the Rass. Like the Ad, the Thamud and the people of Lut, the Ashab ar-Rass were the people of Madyan in the north-west of Arabia. In the district of Al-Qasim of Middle Najad, there was a town called ar-Rass, which had many wells ('*rass*' literally means 'a well'). It was situated between Makkah and Basra (in Iraq). The People of the Rass may have been the people of Prophet Shuayb. They not only refused to listen to the message of their prophet, but they even threw him into a well. They were completely destroyed because of their sins.

▶ **Moral**: Pride makes one foolish and forces one to commit all kinds of sins.

▶ **Key Events**: The message of their Prophet, their destruction.

▶ **See the Quran**: *Al-Furqan* 25:38; *Qaf* 50:12.

▶ **See in this book**: Shuayb and Thamud.

▶ **Study Question**: Who were the Ashab ar-Rass? What did they do to the Prophet Shuayb?

Ashab As-Sabt

Ashab As-Sabt means the Sabbath-breakers. Saturday was made the day of the Sabbath for the Children of Israel from the time of the Prophet Musa (Moses). On the Sabbath day they were asked to do nothing but worship and remember Allah. They had not to do any work, not even fishing. Due to this, on the day of Sabbath, fish came in great numbers to the sea-shore. The young men became greedy and would dig ditches so that the fish would come and be trapped in those ditches. The next day they would collect the fish. In reality, they did not follow Allah's law, but only pretended to. Those who did not observe the law were changed into hateful apes and pigs.

According to a *hadith* of the Prophet Muhammad, those who were changed into apes and pigs could not live for more than three days. They could neither eat food nor give birth to children. The town where this incident happened was ancient Aila (Elath) or the modern Aqaba.

▶ **Moral**: Believers should not use tricks and unfair means to make lawful what has been made unlawful by Allah. It is the spirit which is important along with the action, not just the action.

▶ **Key Events**: Breaking the Sabbath, changing into apes and pigs.

▶ **See the Quran**: *Al-Baqarah* 2:65; *An-Nisaa* 4:47,154; *Al-Araf* 7:163-166; *An-Nahl* 16:124.

▶ **See in this book:** The Children of Israel.

▶ **Study Question**: Why did some of the Children of Israel change into apes and pigs?

How did they break the Sabbath?

Ashab Al-Ukhdud

Ashab Al-Ukhdud is the term used for those who suffered cruelty and were even burnt alive for their faith in Allah. It is said that in 570 A.D. Dhu Nuwas, the last Himayarite king of Yemen, burnt alive Abdullah ibn At-Tamir and others in huge pits filled with fire. These pits were dug to burn those who did not adopt his religion and believed in Allah. Ashab Al-Ukhdud means the human beings who became fuel for the fire pits.

- **Moral**: One should not be cruel to anyone for his different beliefs. A belief or religion should never be forced on anyone.

- **Key Events**: Burning alive the God-fearing men.

- **See the Quran**: *Al-Buruj* 85:4-10.

- **Study Question**: Why were some faithful people burnt alive?

Ashuriyun

Ashuriyun means the Assyrians. They are mentioned in the Quran as the people who defeated the Children of Israel in Palestine in the seventh century B.C.

- **Key Events**: Defeat of the Children of Israel.

- **See the Quran**: *Al-Israa* 17:5.

- **See in this book**: Children of Israel.

- **Study Question**: In what connection are the Ashuriyun mentioned in the Quran?

Asiyah

Asiyah was the believing wife of Firawn (Pharaoh). She believed in Allah and in His supreme power. She also believed that, like everything else, Firawn was also a mere creation of His. She prayed to Allah to

save her from Firawn and his sins and grant her a place in paradise. She was a kind-hearted woman. She picked up the wooden box containing the infant Musa (Moses) from the Nile. She begged Firawn for the child's life and also to be allowed to bring him up. He agreed and she brought him up as her own son in the palace.

The Quran gives her an honourable position along with Maryam. She is an example to all believers.

▶ **Moral**: Allah can grant His Guidance and Grace to anyone. Allah is there for his true believers.

▶ **Key Events**: The saving and bringing up of the Prophet Musa (Moses).

▶ **See the Quran:** *Al-Qasas* 28:9; *At-Tahrim* 66:11.

▶ **See in this book:** Firawn and Musa.

▶ **Relatives**: Husband - Firawn.

▶ **Study Question**: Why does the Quran give an honourable position to Asiyah?

Ayyub

Ayyub (Job) was one of the great prophets of Allah. He was a rich and prosperous man who lived around the 9 th century B.C. in Hawaran, near Damascus in Syria. He had immense faith in Allah and trusted His promises. In spite of being very rich and surrounded with luxuries, he remained a sincere servant of Allah. People felt that the Prophet Ayyub was such a faithful follower of Allah because of his riches and that if his blessings were taken away, he would not remain as faithful and grateful to Allah. Allah put him to a test by destroying all his riches, servants, and family and afflicted him with an illness which lasted for 18 years. In those times of sorrow, his wife also left him. He became very lonely.To make things worse, people who claimed to be his friends said that he was suffering because of his sins.

But he was patient and held fast to his faith in Allah. He continued to be humble, controlled, patient and hopeful. He remembered Allah's mercies and sought His help. Allah was pleased with his steadfastness, constancy and patience. He asked the Prophet Ayyub to strike the ground with his foot. A cool spring of water gushed forth for him to bathe in and this cured his illness. Allah further rewarded him by

doubling his riches and giving him new family and friends. He went on to live to a good old age and saw four generations of his heirs.

The Prophet Ayyub conquered evil with his weapons of humility, patience and unshakeable faith in Allah. No one has ever been as patient, humble, faithful and grateful to Allah as the Prophet Ayyub.

▶ **Moral:** Patience and constancy are also a form of service to Allah if they are due to an active faith in Him.

▶ **Key Events:** The Prophet Ayyub's sufferings, the Prophet Ayyub's restoration.

▶ **See the Quran:** *Al-An'am* 6:84; *Al-Anbiyaa* 21:83-84; *Sad* 38:41-44.

▶ **See in this book:** Dhu'l Kifl.

▶ **Relatives**: Son - The Prophet Dhu'l-Kifl (Bishr)

▶ **Study Question**: Why did Allah destroy the riches and family of the Prophet Ayyub?

What pleased Allah?

Azar

Azar was the father of the Prophet Ibrahim (Abraham). He was a non-believer and an idol-worshipper till he died. When the Prophet Ibrahim was young, he used to question his father about why he worshipped idols when they could not even hear or speak. This used to make Azar angry. When the Prophet Ibrahim grew up, he asked his father to worship Allah, the one and only God, but instead of understanding this truth he forced his son to leave the house. The Prophet Ibrahim left his home in Ur in Iraq and went to Syria.

▶ **Moral**: A sinner will never see or believe the truth, even though he may be closely related to the messengers of Allah.

▶ **Key Events**: The message of the Prophet Ibrahim, the Prophet Ibrahim's departure from his home.

▶ **See the Quran:** *Ash-Shuaraa* 26:86.

▶ **See in this book:** Ibrahim.

▶ **Relatives**: Son - The Prophet Ibrahim

▶ **Study Question**: What did the Prophet Ibrahim asked his father to do?

What was the reaction of Azar?

Aziz

Aziz was the title given to all the high-ranking officials at the court of the ancient Egyptian kings. In the Quran this term is used for Fitfir (Potiphar), the treasurer of Egypt. He had bought young Yusuf (Joseph) from a caravan of merchants who found him in a well, where he had been thrown by his jealous step-brothers to die. He brought up the Prophet Yusuf as his own son. He was a good and just man. His wife was called Zulaykha, she tried to tempt the Prophet Yusuf to lead a sinful life.

▶ **Moral**: No harm can come to those whom Allah saves.

▶ **Key Events**: The buying of the Prophet Yusuf, the false accusations of Zulaykha about the Prophet Yusuf.

▶ **See the Quran**: *Yusuf* 12:30; *Al-Hajj* 22:40.

▶ **See in this book:** Yusuf and Zulaykha.

▶ **Relatives**:   Wife -   Zulaykha

▶ **Study Question**: What sort of a man was the Aziz?

Azrail

Azrail (Azrael) is the angel of death. On receiving orders from Allah, Azrail comes to take a person's soul from his or her body when the time of his or her death comes. The Quran refers to this angel as Malak Al-Mawt (the Angel of Death).

▶ **Moral**: There is an appointed time for everything and everyone has appointed work to do. This is according to Allah's will.

▶ **See the Quran**: *As-Sajdah* 32:11.

▶ **See in this book:** Jibril and Mikal (Michael).

▶ **Study Question**: Who is Azrail?

Baal

Baal was the sun god worshipped in Syria. Baal worship became the court religion of two kings of that time, Ahab (896-874 B.C.) and Ahaziah (874-872 B.C.). During this time, the Prophet Ilyas (Elias, also known as Elijah) asked people to worship only Allah.

▶ **Moral**: Worship God, not His or man's own creations.

▶ **Key Events**: The message of the Prophet Ilyas.

▶ **See in this book**: Ilyas.

▶ **Study Question**: Who was Baal?

Balam

Balam is a term applied to all those to whom Allah's guidance comes, but who turn away from it under Iblis' influence. To be specific, it is said that this term is used for the Children of Israel scholar of great knowledge during the time of the Prophet Musa or possibly for Umayya ibn Abi Salt.

▶ **Moral**: Those who cling to earthly lives and give in to their desires surely become sinners.

▶ **See the Quran**: *Al-Araf* 7:175,176.

▶ **See in this book**: Umayya ibn Abi Salt.

▶ **Study Question**: To whom does the term Balam apply?

Banu Ismail

Banu Ismail is the name fo the descendants of the Prophet Ismail (Ishmael). The Quran also refers to them as Al-Ummiyun, meaning 'the unlettered people'. When the Prophet Ibrahim and the Prophet Ismail were building the Ka'bah, they prayed to Allah to send a prophet with His revelations for the people of this region. Their prayers were heard and after 2500 years the Prophet Muhammad was born among the descendants of the Prophet Ismail.

▶ **Moral**: Allah surely answers the prayers of the believers.

▶ **Key Events**: The building of the Ka'bah, the birth of many prophets, especially the Prophet Muhammad.

▶ **See the Quran**: *Al-Baqarah* 2:129; *Al-Jumua* 62:2.

▶ **See in this book**: Al-Arab, Ismail, Muhammad and Al-Ummiyun

▶ **Study Question**: What did the Prophets Ibrahim and Ismail ask from Allah?

Banu Nadir

Banu Nadir is the name of a Jewish tribe. During the time of the Prophet Muhammad, this tribe was settled near Madinah. Ostensibly, they were the allies of the Madinah Muslims, but secretly they plotted with Makkan pagans under Abu Sufiyan and other enemies of the Muslims to betray them during the Battle of Uhud. They even tried to kill the Prophet Muhammad when he visited them. They thought that no harm would come to them as they lived in fortresses. But when the Muslim army gathered to punish them, their friends did not help them. They left Madinah and went to Syria. Though they deserved punishment, their lives, money and goods were spared.

▶ **Moral**: Justice is not always delivered through punishment. Allah is forgiving and merciful.

▶ **Key Events**: The Battle of Uhud, the departure of the Banu Nadir to Syria.

▶ **See the Quran**: *Al-Hashr* 59:1-17.

▶ **See in this book**: Muhammad.

▶ **Study Question**: Were the Banu Nadir loyal allies of the Madinah Muslims?

Why could they not be saved even in their fortresses?

Banu Qurayza

The Banu Qurayza was a tribe which was settled in the southern outskirts of Madinah during the time of the Prophet Muhammad. This tribe was in alliance with the Prophet to protect the city. But when the Quraysh and their allies came to attack Madinah, the Banu Qurayza left the Muslims and joined the enemy, betraying their own city. However, no fighting took place due to a sandstorm. Later this tribe was surrounded by the Muslim forces for 25 days. Ultimately, the Banu Qurayza had to surrender, giving up everything they had to the

Muslims. Under divine guidance, their men were punished but the women and children were spared.

▶ **Moral**: One should not betray one's own country and should be true to one's promises and commitments.

▶ **Key Events**: Siege of Madinah by the Quraysh, siege by the Muslims of the Banu Qurayza.

▶ **See the Quran**: *Al-Ahzab* 33: 26, 27.

▶ **See in this book**: Muhammad.

▶ **Study Question**: What did the Banu Qurayza do when the Quraysh attacked Madinah?

Bilqis, Queen of Saba

In the sixth century B.C., most of Yemen was ruled by the Queen of Saba (Sheba), whose name was Bilqis. She was a good ruler with a gentle heart and was loyal to her people as they were to her. But all of them worshipped the sun and other heavenly bodies.

The hudhud (hoopoe) informed the Prophet Sulayman (Soloman) about the Queen and her subjects and their being the followers of false gods. The Prophet Sulayman sent a letter inviting her to accept Islam. When the Queen discussed this letter with her council, they advised her to go to war. She did not agree, for she believed that war would only bring about destruction. Instead she sent some gifts to the

Prophet Sulayman, which he refused to accept. Then she went to Jerusalem to meet him. The Prophet Sulayman asked a follower of his to bring her throne before she arrived to meet him. The follower was able to bring the throne because of his great knowledge. Some changes were made in it before she sat on it in the Prophet Sulayman's palace. She realised that it was her throne and was surprised by the power of the Prophet Sulayman.

When she was about to walk into the palace, she thought there was water everywhere, but it was a glass floor with water below it.

When she realized her mistake she saw that in the same way everything she believed and worshipped was false and there was just one reality, and that was Allah, the All-Powerful Creator. She begged for Allah's forgiveness for her sins and submitted herself to Islam.

▶ **Moral**: This is about true and false worship. The Creator should be worshipped rather than His creations.

▶ **Key Events**: The Prophet Sulayman's letter to the Queen of Saba, her visit, her acceptance of Islam.

▶ **See the Quran**: *An-Naml* 27:20-44.

▶ **See in this book**: Ifrit and Sulayman.

▶ **Study Question**: Why did the Queen of Saba object to war?

How did the Queen of Saba become a believer?

Binyamin

Binyamin (Benjamin) was the son of the Prophet Yaqub (Jacob) and the younger brother of the Prophet Yusuf (Joseph). The Prophet Yusuf and Binyamin were from the same mother, Rahil (Rachel). The Prophet Yaqub loved both of them more than his other sons. Binyamin's name is not mentioned in the Quran, but he is indirectly referred to at several points. The Prophet Yusuf asked his step-brothers to bring Binyamin to Egypt during the famine. The Prophet Yusuf revealed his true self to Binyamin and consoled him for all his sufferings because of the evil done by their step-brothers.

▶ **Moral**: Truth and justice always prevail.

▶ **Key Events**: Meeting the Prophet Yusuf.

▶ **See the Quran:** *Yusuf* 12: 8, 69, 87.

▶ **See in this book:** Yahuda, Yaqub and Yusuf.

▶ **Relatives**:
Father   -   The Prophet Yaqub (Jacob)
Brother   -   The Prophet Yusuf (Joseph)
Mother   -   Rahil (Rachel)

▶ **Study Question**: Why is Binyamin mentioned in the Quran?

The Byzantines

Surah 30 of the Quran is called *Ar-Rum* (the Byzantines). On the occasion of the Byzantines being defeated by Persia in 616 A.D., it prophesies victory for the Byzantines in future. This war took place when the Prophet Muhammad had begun his call to accept Islam. The Byzantines were Christians and believed in God's revelations and in prophethood. The Persians were Zoroastrians and worshipped fire and the sun. Therefore, the believers identified themselves with the Byzantines and the unbelievers with the Persians. When news of the Persians' victory spread, the unbelievers mocked the Muslims and said that they would destroy them too in the same way. The Muslims, who were already in a weak and helpless state, felt heart-broken. It was at that time that the Prophet received a highly important revelation about the future victory of the Byzantines.

▶ **Moral**: Allah is Almighty and it is Allah who gives victory to whoever He wills. Nothing is hidden from Allah.

▶ **Key Events**: Defeat of the Byzantines by the Persians, Allah's revelation about the future victory of the Byzantines.

▶ **See the Quran:** *Ar-Rum* 30: 1-5.

▶ **Study Question**: Why did the Muslims feel downhearted at the defeat of the Byzantines?

Children of Israel

The Quran gives a very detailed description of the Children of Israel (Banu Israil), mainly those during the time of the Prophet Musa (Moses). They were Ahl al-Kitab (the People of the Book). The Prophet Musa brought to them special laws, in the form of a book, the Tawrat (Torah). The Arabs and the Children of Israel have a common ancestor in the Prophet Ibrahim (Abraham). Allah bestowed on them many favours but, instead of being thankful to Allah, they became proud and started saying that they were the sons of God and were the chosen ones. In the end only a handful of them followed the teachings of the Prophet Musa. Subsequently they suffered humiliation and misery. The Prophets Dawud (David) and Isa (Jesus) cursed those of the Children of Israel who rejected the faith. The Quran mentions a number of crimes committed by the Children of Israel, but it also praises the group among them who worshipped Allah and did good works.

▶ **Moral**: Arrogance of any kind even if it concerns religion, leads to sin. The Children of Israel were proud of favours from Allah and started believing that they were special which led them into evil.

▶ **Key Events**: The coming of the Prophet Musa and other prophets, the revealing of the Tawrat, the rescue from Firawn, holding the golden calf as an object of worship.

▶ **See the Quran**: *Al-Baqarah* 2:49-53,57,60,61,65,91; *Aal-Imran* 3:12,71,110,113; *An-Nisaa* 4:46,155; *Al-Maidah* 5:13,18,25,41,78; *Al-Hadid* 57:28.

▶ **See in this book:** Ahl al Kitab, Ashab as-Sabt and Musa.

▶ **Study Question**: How did the Children of Israel behave after receiving favours from Allah?

Dawud

The Prophet Dawud (David) and his son, the Prophet Sulayman (Soloman) were kings of the Children of Israel. The Prophet Dawud lived one thousand years before Christ. He was a poor shepherd boy, but the strength of his faith made him destroy Jalut (Goliath), a giant and cruel commander of the Philistine army. This act made him very popular and he was made the king of the Children of Israel.

At the age of forty, he was granted prophethood. Pure faith brings Allah's rewards in many forms and in his case they were power, wisdom and knowledge. The Zabur (Psalms) were revealed to him. He sang the praises of Allah along with nature, the angels and men of God. He also knew the language of the birds. He was the first person who could make armour from iron – an instrument for the defence of

righteousness. He was a good warrior, a great king and a very just judge. In the Quran two incidents are mentioned describing his excellent sense of justice.

▶ **Moral**: Numbers or positions do not matter. The things which matter are faith, determination and the blessing of Allah. Whatever faculties a man has are just gifts from Allah.

▶ **Key Events**: The killing of Jalut, prophethood and becoming the king.

▶ **See the Quran**: *Al-Baqarah* 2:251; *Al-Anam* 6:84; *Al-Anbiyaa* 21: 78-80; *Saba* 34: 10-11; *Sad* 38:17-32.

▶ **See in this book**: Jalut, Queen of Saba, Sulayman and Talut.

▶ **Relatives**:   Son   -   The Prophet Sulayman.

▶ **Study Question**: How did the Prophet Dawud become a king? What were the gifts Allah bestowed upon him?

Dhu'l Kifl

The Prophet Dhu'l Kifl (Ezekiel) ranks with all those prophets who were 'patient' and 'just' men. It is also believed that his real name was Bishr and he was the son of the Prophet Ayyub (Job). He lived in Syria and it is known that his grave lies on the mountain called Jabal Qasiyun. According to some accounts, he was a prophet of the Children of Israel, who was carried away to Babylon by King Nebuchadnezzar after his second attack on Jerusalem in 599 B.C. He was chained and bound and put into prison and for some time he became dumb. He bore all with patience and constancy and continued to preach boldly against the evils in Israel. He denounced false leaders of men, who did not take care of their people but only of themselves.

▶ **Moral**: One can fight against evil with patience and constancy. One should never surrender to evil.

▶ **Key Events**: The taking away of the Prophet Dhu'l Kifl to Babylon.

▶ **See the Quran**: *Al Anbiya* 21: 85; *Sad* 38:48.

▶ **See in this book**: Ayyub.

▶ **Study Question**: Who was the Prophet Dhu'l Kifl?

What did he fight for?

Dhu'l Qarnayn

Dhu'l Qarnayn was a mighty king who is mentioned in the Quran in Surah 18 *Al-Kahf*. Dhu'l Qarnayn's deeds illustrate the qualities of a good king. Some say he was Alexander the Great, others point towards

Cyrus the Great of Persia, while yet others say he was a pre-historic Himyarite king. He was a just and righteous ruler.

There are three episodes in which he figures in the Quran. The first episode is about his rule over unruly people. He protected the weak and punished the unlawful. He possessed great power and availed of every opportunity to do justice and spread righteousness. However, he believed that his power was given to him by Allah. He gave equal opportunities to the rich and poor to be virtuous and to do good. In the second episode he encountered a primitive and different people. He did not interfere in their lives and left them in peace. He was wise and tolerant to people. He knew his own position and believed in living and letting others live. Finally he met a people who were different but not totally primitive. They were skilled in the working of metals. Peace-loving and hardworking people, they were troubled by attacks from the wild tribes of Yajuj and Majuj (Gog and Magog).

Dhu'l-Qarnayn helped them to raise an iron wall to check their attacks. In spite of all his efforts, he claimed no credit for himself. He told them that it was Allah who had provided the ways and means by which they could be helped and protected.

▶ **Moral**: After conquering a major part of the then inhabited world and building an iron wall, Dhu'l Qarnayn lost none of his humility. He gave the entire credit for these feats to the blessing of Allah. A ruler should use his power which Allah has given to him to fulfill his duties and responsibilties towards his people. He should protect them and provide them with equal opportunities.

▶ **Key Events**: Ruling the unruly people, meeting primitive but powerful people and then different but hardworking people, making an iron wall.

▶ **See the Quran**: *Al-Kahf* 18: 83-101.

▶ **See in this book**: Yajuj and Majuj.

▶ **Study Question**: Who is an ideal king?

What qualities of an ideal king do the three episodes in the life of Dhu'l Qarnayn highlight?

Firawn

Firawn (Pharaoh) was not the name of any particular king of Egypt but the title of the Amalekite kings who ruled ancient Egypt. The Quran refers to the cruel Firawn who ruled during the time of the Prophet Musa (Moses). Historians are certain, that he was Merenptah.

He was a proud, selfish, cruel and false leader. He believed he was the one and only god and forced everyone to believe in him and worship him. This was the state religion along with magic and the worship of animals and the forces of nature. Those who did not follow it were punished. He believed in the lies he had created and refused to see the truth. Firawn was proud of his power, material civilization and race. He did not fulfill his duties as a ruler and was grievously cruel to the Children of Israel because they belonged to a different race. They were not treated as equal to the Egyptians. He forced all kind of cruelties on the Children of Israel. They were made to do hard labour and no good was ever done for them. He even cunningly ordered that all the male children of the Israelites' be killed, leaving the females available for marriage to the Egyptians, so that the Israelites' race would thus end. When his magicians were so impressed by the Prophet Musa's miracles that they declared their faith in Allah, he could not believe it; his pride was hurt. He first angrily warned them and then had them killed in the cruelest ways. He wanted to destroy the Children of Israel, but Allah's plan was to protect them as they were weak. Allah also made them the followers of His faith under the guidance of the Prophet Musa.

Firawn did not believe in Allah or in His Prophet, and he mocked the Prophet Musa and his followers, who were poor. Firawn and his people were mighty, learned in science, art, organization and power.

They were prosperous and firmly established. They broke the laws of Allah. However, the forces of man are no match for the power of Allah. Firawn and his people were struck by plagues. Finally, they drowned in the sea when they were chasing the Prophet Musa and the Children of Israel, who were saved by Allah. The Quran says that Firawn's body was saved as a sign to the mankind. 1400 years after his death his body was discovered in 1898 in the form of a mummy.

▶ **Moral:** A king should not force his beliefs and religion on his people. Neither should he use religion to exploit and control his people. However mighty a person may be, he cannot break the laws of Allah without inviting His punishment.

▶ **Key Events:** The coming of the Prophet Musa, plagues, the drowning of Firawn.

▶ **See the Quran:** *Al-Baqarah* 2:49-50; *Al-A'raf* 7:103-137; *Yunus* 10:75-92; *Al-Qasas* 28:38; *Gafir* 40:28-44; *Ad-Dukhan* 44:17-33;

Al-Qamar 54:41-42; *At-Tahrim* 66:11; *Al-Haqqa* 69:9; *Al-Muzzammil* 73:16; *An-Nazi'at* 79:24; *Al-Buruj* 85:17-20; *Al-Fajr* 89:10-14.

▶ **See in this book:** Asiyah, Harun, Haman, Musa, Qarun, Sahara Firawn and Shaman.

▶ **Study Question**: Who was Firawn?

What were Firawn's beliefs about religion?

What was the end of Firawn and his people?

What should a good ruler not do?

Habil and Qabil

Habil (Abel) and Qabil (Cain) were the two sons of the Prophet Adam and Hawwa. Habil, the younger of the two, was a shepherd, while Qabil was a farmer. One day Habil and Qabil made offerings to Allah. Habil's offering was accepted but Qabil's was rejected because he was proud, selfish and did not fear Allah. Instead of realising his mistake, he got, jealous and felt hatred for Habil because his offerings were accepted by Allah. Qabil threatened to kill his younger brother. But Habil who was innocent and unselfish did not fight. Though he was equally strong, he said that he would not fight back because he feared Allah. He also tried to explain to his brother that this way he would just add to his sins and would suffer in hell. Qabil's pride and jealousy

blinded him with anger and this led him to murder Habil. Later on when Qabil's anger cooled down he felt sorry and ashamed of his deed. He buried Habil's body under the earth.

The Quran says: 'If anyone killed a human being—except as a punishment for murder or other corruption in the land, it shall be as if he had killed the whole of humanity. And whoever saved a human life, shall be looked upon as if he had saved all mankind.' (5:32).

▶ **Moral**: Pride, selfishness, jealousy and anger lead to evil. Killing another is the greatest sin.

▶ **Key Events**: Qabil's killing Habil.

▶ **See the Quran**: *Al-Maidah* 5:27-31.

▶ **See in this book**: Adam.

▶ **Relatives**:

Father	-	Adam
Mother	-	Hawwa

Hajar

Hajar (Hagar) was the wife of the Prophet Ibrahim (Abraham) and the mother of the Prophet Ismail (Ishmael). When Ismail was born to her, the Prophet Ibrahim was ordered by Allah to go towards Makkah to build the Ka'bah as it was isolated and fit to be a centre for prayer and praise of Allah. The Prophet Ibrahim immediately left along with Hajar and their infant son, Ismail. Near Mount As-Safa he left the son and the mother. Later, when Ismail was thirsty, he cried for water. There was no water around. But Hajar was firm in her faith in Allah.

She believed that Allah would not let them die. She ran several times between the Mounts of As-Safa and Al-Marwah in search of water. There was not a single drop of water to drink. Then Allah made a spring well up beneath the feet of Ismail. Later this spring became famous as the well of Zam Zam. Allah was so pleased with Hajar's faith in Him that He made it compulsory for all those who go on the pilgrimage (Hajj) to repeat her actions.

▶ **Moral**: Allah never disappoints those who have complete faith in Him.

▶ **Key Events**: Coming to Makkah, the search for water, the gushing forth of the spring.

▶ **See the Quran**: *Ibrahim* 14:37.

▶ **See in this book**: Ibrahim and Ismail

▶ **Relatives**:
Husband   -   Prophet Ibrahim
Son   -   Prophet Ismail

▶ **Study Question**: What was the name of the spring which gushed forth beneath the feet of Ismail?

What do we understand about the nature of Hajar?

Why was Allah happy with Hajar?

Haman

Haman was a minister and close advisor of Firawn (Pharaoh). He is mentioned several times in the Quran. Once while making fun of the Prophet Musa (Moses), Firawn even asked Haman to build up a tower, so that he could reach heaven and see the God of the Prophet Musa. Firawn and his men, like Haman, did not believe in Allah or the Hereafter and refused to accept that every deed has a result—good or evil.

▶ **Moral**: Anyone who thinks or supports the idea that he is stronger than Allah will surely come to an evil end. It is only pride and foolishness which make one think in that way.

▶ **Key Events**: The Prophet Musa's message, Firawn asking to build the tower.

▶ **See the Quran**: *Al-Qasas* 28:8, 38; *Al-Ankabut* 29:39; *Gafir* 40: 36-37.

▶ **See in this book**: Firawn, Musa and Qarun.

▶ **Study Question**: Who was Haman and what did Firawn ask him to do?

What were the beliefs of Firawn and Haman?

Hannah

Hannah (Anna/Anne) was the mother of Maryam (Mary). Her husband was Imran (Amran). She was God-fearing and had great faith in Allah. Before the birth of Maryam she had prayed to Allah, vowing that she would send her child to the service of Allah in the temple. Hannah hoped for a male child; under the Mosaic laws a female child could not be devoted to the temple service. But she was still not disappointed when Maryam was born, for she knew that Allah's plan was better than any wishes of hers. Allah took care of Maryam and later she gave birth to the miracle child, the Prophet Isa (Jesus), as desired by Allah.

▶ **Moral**: Man makes his own plans but Allah's plans are better. One should have firm faith in Allah and believe that whatever He does for man is in his best interest.

▶ **Key Events**: Birth of Maryam.

▶ **See the Quran**: *Aal-Imran* 3: 35-37.

▶ **See in this book**: Imran, Isa, Maryam, Yahya and Zakariyya.

▶ **Relatives**:

Husband	-	Imran
Daughter	-	Maryam
Grandson	-	Prophet Isa.

▶ **Study Question**: Why was Hannah not unhappy when she gave birth to Maryam instead of a male child as earlier desired by her?

Harun

The Prophet Harun (Aaron) was an elder brother of the Prophet Musa (Moses). When the Prophet Musa was asked by Allah to go to the court of Firawn (Pharaoh) to give him the message of true religion, he prayed to Him for courage. He also asked for his brother Harun's support in his mission, because he spoke with a stammer. Allah granted him this request. In all his missions the Prophet Harun was with him.

When the Prophet Musa went to Mount Tur for 40 days, he left the Children of Israel in his brother's care. But most of the Children of Israel were wrongdoers. They made a golden calf and started worshipping it. They did not listen to the Prophet Harun. When the Prophet Musa returned, he thought that all this had happened because the Prophet Harun had failed in his duties. In the end when the Children of Israel did not respond to the call of the Prophet Musa, he understood and prayed to Allah in his disappointment to save him and his brother from the wicked people. The Prophet Harun remained with the Prophet Musa till he died at the age of 122 years. Eleven months later the Prophet Musa also died.

▶ **Moral**: Weak souls, even those who come to believe in Allah's truth, create mischief whenever they have the opportunity to do so. Their faith is nominal. They are as bad as arrogant and proud people.

▶ **Key Events**: Message of the Prophet Musa, the Children of Israel worshipping of the golden calf in the absence of the Prophet Musa.

▶ **See the Quran:** *Al Maidah* 5:25; *Al-Araf* 7:142,148; *Ta-Ha* 20:25-34; 91, 94; *Al-Qasas* 28: 34.

▶ **See in this book:** Firawn, Musa, As-Samiri and Umm Musa.

▶ **Relatives**:

Brother	-	The Prophet Musa
Father	-	Imran
Mother	-	Yukabid

▶ **Study Question**: Why did the Prophet Musa ask for the Prophet Harun's help in his mission?

What misunderstanding did the Prophet Musa have with the Prophet Harun?

Harut and Marut

The Children of Israel believed in the will of Allah and in their books. But later they started engaging in certain evil practices, like using magic for their own benefit. Moreover, they justified this practice by saying, wrongly, that they had learnt it from the Prophet Sulayman (Solomon). Before destroying them, Allah tried to test and warn them through Harut and Marut, the good men, who lived in Babylon (Iraq), a very ancient seat of science, especially of astronomy. Harut and Marut gave their knowledge to all who came to them, but with the warning that it should not fall into the hands of evil men. They could see that with this knowledge people could become arrogant and thereby sinners and could also use it to harm others.

The evil ones started creating discord between men and women with this knowledge. But their power was limited. It could not affect the true believers of Allah. Eventually the evil-doers suffered most from it.

▶ **Moral**: Allah has given us free will. When one has knowledge one can easily use it either to the benefit or to the detriment of society.

▶ **Key Events**: The use of magic, the destruction of evil-doers.

▶ **See the Quran:** *Al-Baqarah* 2:102-103.

▶ **See in this book:** The Children of Israel.

▶ **Study Question:** How should knowledge be used?

Hawariyyun

Hawariyyun (the apostles) were the disciples of the Prophet Isa (Jesus). When the Children of Israel rejected him, he cried out for help for the cause of Allah. A few of them said that they believed in

Allah and followed his messenger (the Prophet Isa). The Quran praises their role and asks other believers to follow them. Upon their demand Allah sent down a table spread with food from Heaven at their request. But Allah warned them that now, if they rejected the faith they would be punished more than other sinners.

▶ **Moral**: If we seek Allah's help, we must first help Allah's cause which means dedicating ourselves to Him entirely. A little faith or seeing and believing, in fact, is no faith at all.

▶ **Key Events**: The Prophet Isa asking for help, the miracle of the table of food.

▶ **See the Quran**: *Aal-Imran* 3:52-53; *Al-Maidah* 5:112-115; *As-Saff* 61:14.

▶ **See in this book**: Ahl al-Kitab, An-Nasara and Isa

▶ **Study Question**: Who were the *Hawariyyun*?

What did the *Hawariyyun* ask for from the Prophet Isa?

The Hawazin

The Hawazin was one of the major tribes who, along with the Thaqif, organised an attack on the Muslims during the times of the Prophet Muhammad. They assembled their army at Taif, the city of al-Lat and a centre of paganism. The armies met the battle of Hunain at the end of January 630 AD. This happened after the conquest of Makkah in the year 8 A.H. (After Hijrah). The Muslims defeated the rebels.

▶ **Moral**: Only defensive war is allowed in Islam.

▶ **Key Events**: The Battle of Hunain.

▶ **See in this book**: Muhammad

▶ **Study Question**: What is the significance of the battle of Hunain?

Hud

The Prophet Hud was sent by Allah to the people of Ad. He was the first person to speak Arabic. The Ad people were descendants of Iram, one of the grandsons of the Prophet Nuh (Noah). The Ad's terrain in Southern Arabia stretched from Umman, ancient Yemen, at the mouth of the Arabian Gulf to the southern end of the Red Sea. Iram was their capital, which had many buildings with tall pillars. At that time there was no city like it. Its inhabitants were great builders and made good irrigation canals in the vast tracts of sands. The Ad, accomplished in the arts and sciences were very cultured people. In the beginning they followed the religion of the Prophet Nuh. But like any material civilization they became proud, obstinate and fell into evil ways. They were cruel in the use of their power. They stopped thinking that

everything they had was only a gift from Allah, and started worshipping false gods. The Prophet Hud asked the Ad to give up their wrong and cruel ways and to worship Allah. They blamed the Prophet Hud for not giving them clear proof of Allah. They mocked at him and said that maybe the powers of their gods had made him foolish.

As a warning, Allah sent a terrible drought to their land. For almost three years, there was no rain. But they continued to sin. Instead of turning to Allah for forgiveness, they kept praying to false gods and performing superstitious acts. When the Prophet Hud again asked them to give up their wrong ways or suffer Allah's punishment, they challenged him to bring it down upon them. When a storm approached them, they thought it was only a cloud bringing rain, which would end their troubles. But it was a storm which lasted seven nights and eight days and completely destroyed them, because they had broken Allah's laws. If they had obeyed Allah and His laws of righteousness, they would have become more prosperous and powerful.

The Prophet Hud and those who had faith and trust in Allah were saved and they were later known as the Thamud. The Prophet Hud's tomb is on the hillock called Hadramawt about 90 miles north of Mukalla in Yemen.

▶ **Moral**: The punishment for evil is certain, but only Allah knows when it will come. When one becomes proud and breaks the laws of Allah, he invites His punishment.

▶ **Key Events**: The message of the Prophet Hud, drought and storm.

▶ **See the Quran:** *Al-Araf* 7: 65-72, *Hud* 11:50-60, *Ash-Shuaraa* 26:123-140, *Al-Ahqaf* 46:21-26.

▶ **See in this book:** Ad.

▶ **Study Question:** Why were the people of Ad destroyed?

How were they destroyed? Explain briefly.

Ibrahim

After the Prophet Nuh (Noah), Ibrahim (Abraham) was selected by Allah to be His prophet. He was born in the ancient city of Ur in Iraq, about 300 kms away from Baghdad. In the beginning, he preached the message of the oneness of God, truth and unity in his own country,

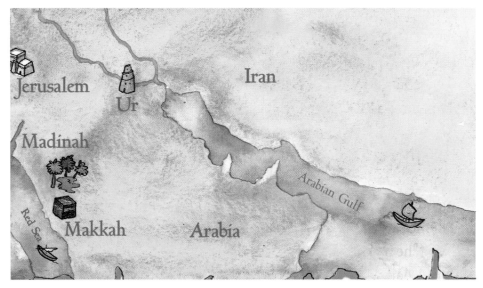

and later in Syria, Palestine and Egypt also. Finally, he settled down in Arabia. He is buried in the town of al-Khalil near Jerusalem. From the heirs of his elder son, the Prophet Ismail (Ishmael), the Muslims were born and the Jews and Christians were the heirs of his younger son, the Prophet Ishaq (Isaac).

The Prophet Ibrahim was born among the Chaldeans who had great knowledge of the stars and other heavenly bodies. They also worshipped them. They were idol worshippers. Even as a child he wondered why his people worshipped lifeless and powerless idols or stars. When he questioned his father, Azar, or his people, they scolded him and said that they would continue to do what their fathers did. The Prophet Ibrahim wanted them to think for themselves and realise that there was only one God who was the Creator of the world. One day, to explain his message that they were mere creations, he destroyed all the idols except the biggest one. But they did not see the truth and instead became angry with him and tried to burn him alive. His immense faith in Allah saved him and Allah made the fire cool and safe for him.

Iraq was then ruled by Namrud (Nimrod), a cruel king, who was worshipped as a god by his people. He was angry with the Prophet Ibrahim and his message and argued with him that he was all-powerful. Namrud said that even he could give life or death like God. But when questioned by the Prophet Ibrahim if he could bring the sun out from the west, he had no answer. The Prophet Ibrahim said that everything Namrud had was a gift from Allah. The Prophet Ibrahim's message challenged the authority of the king and this angered him. The king, the people and his father grew very angry with him and turned against him. He went away to Syria with his wife and nephew, the Prophet Lut (Lot).

After his elder son Ismail was born to his wife, Hajar (Hagar), Allah asked him to go to Makkah. One night the Prophet Ibrahim dreamt that he was sacrificing his son, Ismail, at Allah's behest. When he told his son about his dream, he agreed to be sacrificed. They went to Mina and, on the way, Iblis (Satan) tried to stop them, but they threw stones at him. When the Prophet Ibrahim was about to sacrifice his son, the Angel Jibril (Gabriel) stopped him by replacing Ismail with a ram, which was then sacrificed. Allah was pleased with the Prophet Ibrahim because of his readiness to do His bidding. He asked believers to observe this day as Id-al-Adha (the feast of sacrifice). As desired by Allah, the Prophets Ibrahim and Ismail built the Ka'bah, the House of Allah, in Makkah. While building it, they prayed to Allah to send a messenger after them to teach people the Book, the truth, and wisdom and save them from all evil. Their prayer was granted, and after 2,500 years, the Prophet Muhammad was born among the descendants of the Prophet Ismail.

Allah asked them to clean His House so that believers could worship Him there. The structure which is known as the "standing place of Ibrahim" (Maqam Ibrahim) still exists near the Ka'bah. Allah ordered believers to consider this spot as a place of prayer.

One day some angels came to him and foretold the birth of his second son Ishaq (Isaac) by his barren wife, Sarah. The Prophet Ishaq was a gift (*nafilah*) given to the Prophet Ibrahim.

The Prophet Ibrahim is known as the friend of Allah and also as *hanif*—true in faith. Believers are asked to follow in his footsteps. The Quran tells the Prophet Muhammad that 'the righteous' belong to the community of Ibrahim.

▶ **Moral**: Allah's message is the same in all ages. Allah is always there to help His believers. One should give oneself completely to Allah, which means we should give up everything if Allah requires it. Only faith in Allah can save a believer in both the worlds.

▶ **See the Quran**: *Al-Baqarah* 2:125-127,129, 135, 172,258; *Aal-Imran* 3:96-97; *Al-Anam* 6:74-84; *Hud* 11:69-76; *Ibrahim* 14:35-41; *An-Nahl* 16:120-123; *Maryam* 19:41-50; *Al-Anbiyaa* 21:69, 72, 51-71; *Ash-Shuaraa* 26:86,69,82-104; *Al-Ankabut* 29:26-27; *As-Saffat* 37:102-111; *An-Najm* 53:37; *Al-Mumthana* 60:4; *Al-A'la* 87:19.

▶ **Key Events**: Inviting people to true faith, migration, birth of Ismail and Ishaq, building of the Ka'bah.

▶ **See in this book:** Hajar, Ishaq, Ismail, Namrud and Sarah.

▶ **Relatives**:

Father	-	Azar
Wife	-	Hajar
Wife	-	Sarah
Son	-	The Prophet Ismail
Son	-	The Prophet Ishaq
Nephew	-	The Prophet Lut

▶ **Study Question**: Why is the Prophet Ibrahim called the father of three religions – Judaisim, Christianity and Islam?

What religion did the Prophet Ibrahim's people practice?

Why is Id-al-Adha observed?

What did the Prophets Ibrahim and Ismail pray to Allah for?

Idris

The Prophet Idris was probably born before the Prophet Nuh (Noah). He was a rich and prosperous man with a good position in society. He was humble and kept himself in touch with his people and was respected by them. He was sincere and truthful and that was the particular quality of his constancy and patience. The Prophet Idris was the first person to write with a pen. He lived for 365 years. Some identify him with Enoch of the Bible.

▶ **Moral**: One should always be humble, whatever one's position in life, the more so when one is rich.

▶ **See the Quran**: *Maryam* 19:56-57; *Al-Anbiyaa* 21:85.

▶ **Study Question**: Who was Idris?

What was he known for?

Ifrit

Ifrit was a large powerful jinn mentioned in the Quran who offered to bring the throne of Bilqis, the Queen of Saba (Sheba), to the Prophet Sulayman (Solomon), even before he could rise from his seat. But instead the Prophet Sulayman chose one who had deep knowledge of the Book, who then brought it in the twinkling of an eye. The Prophet

Sulayman was thankful to Allah for the correct choice he had made and also for the power he posessed.

▶ **Moral**: Knowledge is more powerful and effective than mere physical strength.

▶ **Key Events**: Bringing of the throne.

▶ **See the Quran**: *An-Naml* 27:39, 40.

▶ **See in this book**: Bilqis and Sulayman.

▶ **Study Question**: Who was Ifrit?

Did he bring the throne of the Queen of Saba?

Ilyas

The Prophet Ilyas (Elias, also known as Elijah) belonged to the group of prophets who are called righteous in the Quran. They were solely preachers of truth.

He lived during the reigns of Kings Ahab (896-874 B.C.) and Ahaziah (874-872 B.C.) in the northern kingdom of Israel. King Ahab had married a princess of Sidon, Jezebel. She was a wicked woman who led her husband into worshipping Baal, the sun god. Both the kings and their subjects worshipped Baal and also the powers of nature. The Prophet Ilyas asked them to worship the real and one and only God—Allah. He also denounced the sins of the kings and, therefore,

had to leave to save his life. His task was continued by the Prophet Alyasa (Elisha).

▶ **Moral**: Wicked people worship false gods, which suits their selfish ways of living.

▶ **Key Events**: Message of the Prophet Ilyas.

▶ **See the Quran**: *Al-An'am* 6:85; *As-Saffat* 37:123-132.

▶ **See in this book:** Alyasa and Baal.

▶ **Study Question**: Why was Prophet Ilyas called the 'Prophet of the desert'?

What was the message of the Prophet Ilyas?

Why did the Prophet Ilyas leave?

Imran

The Quran mentions two different men, both called Imran (Amran). The first Imran was the father of the Prophets Musa (Moses) and Harun (Aaron). The other Imran mentioned in the Quran was the husband of Hannah, the mother of Maryam.

▶ **Moral:** All men of faith in Allah form one family.

▶ **Key Events:** Birth of the Prophets Harun, Musa and Maryam.

▶ **See the Quran:** *Aal- Imran* 3:33, 35.

▶ **See in this book:** Hannah, Harun, Maryam and Musa.

▶ **Relatives:** Imran (1) Wife - Yukabid
Sons - Musa, Harun.
Daughter - Hannah
Imran (2) Wife - Hannah
Daughter - Maryam
Grandson - Isa ibn Maryam (Jesus)

▶ **Study Question:** What was the name of the father of Maryam?

Isa ibn Maryam

The Prophet Isa (Jesus), one of the great prophets, was born to Maryam (Mary) in Bethlehem. He lived and grew up in An-Nasiriya (Nazareth). Allah had chosen Maryam and purified her among all the women of the world to give birth to the Prophet Isa without any normal conception. He was a miracle-child and lived a life of miracles until he was raised up to heaven.

He started his mission as a child in the arms of his mother. He defended his mother when she was accused of being unchaste. He was blessed with the power to work miracles in order to convince people of the truth of his mission. He cured the blind and the lepers and brought people back to life. But even then, the people of Israel did not believe in him and mocked him. Some of his disciples also did not believe in him completely and asked for miracles to have their minds set at rest about his message. The Prophet Isa confirmed the scriptures sent before him, the Tawrat (Torah) and revealed the Injil (Gospel) to them. He also gave news of a Prophet who would come

after him and his name would be Ahmad. He asked his followers not to let themselves be lost in the pleasures of this world, but to believe in Allah, the one true God, and to follow His laws.

The Prophet Isa asked his followers not to associate anyone with God. The Prophet Isa acknowledged that he was mortal and that his knowledge was limited like that of a mortal. All the powers he had were gifts from Allah. The most honoured of the prophets of Allah are also only men. All power belongs to Allah, and not to any human being. The Quran calls the Prophet Isa the son of Maryam and a messenger of Allah.

The Prophet Isa continued his mission for several years, but only a few answered his call. The people of Israel wanted to kill him. But Allah saved him and raised him up to heaven. They crucified another

man who was made to appear like him. The Prophet Muhammad said that the Prophet Isa would return to earth as a 'just ruler'.

▶ **Moral**: Allah is one; His message is one; yet the evil ways of people transform truth into falsehood, religion into superstition.

▶ **Key Events**: Birth of the Prophet Isa, miracles, raising of the Prophet Isa to heaven

▶ **See the Quran**: *Aal-Baqarah* 2:140; *Aal-Imran* 3:45-53,55-59; *An-Nisaa* 4:153-161, 171; *Al-Maidah* 5:7,18, 41, 42, 46, 73, 110-118; *Al-Anam* 6:85; *At-Tauba* or *Baraat* 9:30; *Ar-Rad*13:38, *Maryam* 19:22-33; *Al-Muminun* 23:50; *Ash-Shuaraa* 26:197; *Al-Qasas* 28:53; *Az-Zukhruf* 43:61; *As-Saff* 61:6, 14.

▶ **See in this book**: Ahl al-Kitab, Hawariyyun, Hannah, Maryam, An-Nasara, Yahya and Zakariyya.

▶ **Relatives**:

Mother	-	Maryam
Grandfather	-	Imran
Grandmother	-	Hannah
Uncle	-	the Prophet Zakariyya
Cousin	-	the Prophet Yahya

▶ **Study Question**: What were the gifts given to the Prophet Isa by Allah?
What was the message of the Prophet Isa?

Ishaq

The Prophet Ishaq (Isaac) was the younger son of the Prophet Ibrahim (Abraham) and Sarah. He was the younger brother of the Prophet Ismail (Ishmael). He lived in Palestine. He was a forefather of the line of prophets starting from the Prophet Yaqub (Jacob) and ending with the Prophet Isa (Jesus). He was a truthful and righteous man.

The Prophet Ishaq's birth was foretold by the angels to the Prophet Ibrahim when they were on their way to destroy the people of the Prophet Lut, for their sins. When he was born, both the Prophet Ibrahim and his wife, Sarah were in old age. The birth of the Prophet Ishaq was a gift (*nafila*) given by Allah to the the Prophet Ibrahim. It was a gift for the display of his faith in Allah by readily agreeing to sacrifice his only son, the Prophet Ismail, at Allah's behest.

▶ **Moral**: Allah rewards His faithful followers with beautiful gifts. Their generations are blessed.

▶ **Key Events**: Birth of Ishaq.

▶ **See the Quran**: *Al-An'am* 6:84; *Maryam* 19:49, 50; *Al-Anbiyaa* 21:72; *As Saffat* 37:112-113.

▶ **See in this book**: Ibrahim, Ismail, Sarah and Yaqub.

▶ **Relatives**:

Father	-	the Prophet Ibrahim
Mother	-	Sarah
Brother	-	the Prophet Ismail
Son	-	the Prophet Yaqub

▶ **Study Question**: Why was the Prophet Ishaq a gift from Allah?

Ismail

The Prophet Ismail (Ishmael) was the elder son of the Prophet Ibrahim (Abraham) and his wife Hajar (Hagar). His younger brother was Prophet Ishaq. The Prophet Ismail was the ancestor of the Prophet Muhammad. He was still an infant when the Prophet Ibrahim was asked to go to Makkah where hardly anyone lived. When Hajar was alone and her little son cried for water, she ran between the mountains of As-Safa and Al-Marwa seven times, searching for water. Allah was pleased with her belief in Him and a spring gushed out beneath the

feet of the Prophet Ismail, which was later called Zam Zam.

One day the Prophet Ibrahim dreamt of sacrificing his son and, when he told this to his son, he willingly agreed for it. It was a sacrifice demanded from both the father and the son. It was a test of their will. Allah was pleased with them and sent a ram to be sacrificed instead of the Prophet Ismail. He helped his father in building the Ka'bah and later also in cleaning it.

▶ **Moral**: Allah is always there to help and protect believers; self-sacrifice in the service of Allah is the supreme act in life. Allah rewards those who make sacrifices.

▶ **Key Events**: Gushing out of Zam Zam, dream of sacrifice, building of the Ka'bah.

▶ **See the Quran:** *Al-Baqarah* 2:125-129; *Al-An'am* 6:86; *Ibrahim* 14:37; *Maryam* 19:54-55; *Al-Anbiyaa* 21:85; *As-Saffat* 37:102-111.

▶ **See in this book:** Hajar, Ibrahim, Ishaq and Muhammad.

▶ **Relatives:**
Father   -   the Prophet Ibrahim
Mother   -   Hajar
Brother   -   the Prophet Ishaq

▶ **Study Question:** What did the Prophet Ibrahim dream?

What did he do after that dream?

How did Allah reward the Prophet Ibrahim?

Jalut

Jalut (Goliath) was a giant Philistine. He was a commander of their army, who was very cruel to the Children of Israel and made their lives miserable. He was killed by the young Prophet Dawud (David).

▶ **Moral:** Mighty men are destroyed if they are cruel and break the laws of Allah.

▶ **Key Events:** Jalut's cruelty and his killing by the Prophet Dawud.

▶ **See the Quran:** *Al-Baqarah* 2:249-251.

▶ **See in this book:** Dawud and Talut.

▶ **Study Question**: What is the result of being cruel and breaking the laws of Allah?

Jibril

Jibril (Gabriel) was one of the four angels favoured by Allah who brought Allah's revelations to His prophets. The Prophet Muhammad received the revelations from Allah through Jibril. The first time when he appeared in a visible form was at Jabal al-Nur (the Mountain of Light), where he brought the first revelation, beginning with *Surah* 96 *Iqra*. Generally he appeared in human form, but the Prophet Muhammad also saw him 'in the clear sky' spreading his wings from east to west, when he came very near to him though still in the air. Jibril also took him on the Night Journey and the Ascent to Heaven (*miraj*). It was on the *miraj* that he saw Jibril near the *sidra* tree (lote tree) and at the *Jannat al-Mawa* (Gardens of Refuge), beyond which no one can go.

Once in Taif, people insulted the Prophet and even threw stones at him, making him bleed from head to toe. Jibril then appeared with Malak al-Jibal (the Angel of the mountains) to take his permission to destroy the people of Taif. But the Prophet Muhammad refused and prayed for these people to be guided.

The People of the Book during the time of Prophet Muhammad ridiculed the idea that Jibril brought down Allah's revelation to the

Prophet Muhammad. For them Jibril was an angel of death and punishment and, therefore, an enemy. They believed that Mikal (the Angel Michael) was their friend. It was very foolish of them that they believe in one angel and not in the others. It showed their lack of belief in the angels, the prophets and Allah. Jibril holds a very honourable position in the Quran, in which he is called *Ruh al-Qudus* (the Holy Spirit), or *Ruh al-Amin* (the Faithful Spirit) and *Rasul Karim* (the Honourable Messenger).

▶ **Moral**: You cannot believe in just parts of a religion. The verses of the Quran are reasonable and clear. Allah's signs are clear, but sinners refuse to understand them.

▶ **Key Events**: The bringing of revelations to the Prophet Muhammad.

▶ **See the Quran:** *Al-Baqarah* 2:87, 97, 98; *Ash-Shuaraa* 26:193; *An-Najm* 53:5-10, 13-15; *At-Tahrim* 66:4; *At-Takwir* 81:19-21, 23.

▶ **See in this book:** Mikal and Muhammad.

▶ **Study Question:** Which was the first revelation received by the Prophet Muhammad?

In what forms did the Prophet Muhammad see Jibril?

What had happened in Taif?

Why did the People of the Book ridicule the notion that Jibril brought down Allah's revelation to the Prophet Muhammad?

What are the different names by which Jibril is referred to in the Quran?

Ka'b ibn Malik

Ka'b ibn Malik was one of the companions of the Prophet Muhammad. During the campaign of Tabuk, some true Muslims were not able to join the Prophet Muhammad. Their reasons were not ill-will but thoughtlessness and human weakness. After he returned, the hypocrites gave him many excuses for not going. But Ka'b ibn Malik, Marara ibn ar-Rabi and Hilal ibn Umayya immediately told him the true reasons. The Prophet did not say anything but stopped all interaction with them for a long time. This made them realise their failure in performing their duties and they felt very sorry about it. In

all humbleness they prayed to Allah for His forgiveness. After 50 days a verse of the Quran (*At-Tawba* 9:119) was revealed to the Prophet in which Allah forgave them.

▶ **Moral**: Allah forgives those who truly feel sorry for their misdeeds.

▶ **Key Events**: Not going for the campaign, realising their mistake.

▶ **See the Quran**: *At-Tawba* 9:118-119.

▶ **Study Question**: Why did Ka'b ibn Malik not join in the campaign of Tabuk?

Did he realise his mistake?

Did Allah forgive him?

Kalab

The Prophet Musa wanted to take the Children of Israel into the holy land, but they refused to enter because they were scared of its inhabitants, the giant Amalekites. The Children of Israel were afraid to fight with them, therefore, they disobeyed their prophet. He sent Kalab (Caleb) and Yusha bin Nun (Joshua), who had the faith and the courage to go secretly and see the actual situation there. They suggested an immediate entry after taking the necessary precautions and making all due preparations. But they said that they must put their trust in Allah for victory.

▶ **Moral**: Faith in Allah gives true courage.

▶ **Key Events**: Fear of entering the holy land.

▶ **See the Quran:** *Al-Maida* 5:23.

▶ **See in this book:** The Children of Israel, Musa and Yusha bin Nun.

▶ **Study Question**: Why did the Children of Israel refuse to enter the holy land?

What did Kalab and Yusha bin Nun suggest?

Kanan

Kanan was the unbelieving son of the the Prophet Nuh (Noah). The Prophet Nuh asked his son to come with him in his Ark at the time of the great flood and not to stay back with the unbelievers. But he did not listen to his father and instead climbed up a mountain peak to save himself. Like other unbelievers he had more faith in material things than in Allah. Subsequently, the mountain peaks also became submerged in water and he was drowned along with all the other unbelievers.

▶ **Moral**: The unbelievers refuse to listen to Allah, but have great faith in material things.

▶ **Key Events**: The message of the Prophet Nuh, the flood.

▶ **See the Quran**: *Hud* 11:42-46 *Al-Muminun* 23:28.

▶ **See in this book:** Nuh and wife of Nuh.

▶ **Relatives:**   Father   -   The Prophet Nuh.

    Mother   -   Waliya

▶ **Study Question:** Why did Kanan climb up the mountain peak? Did he save himself?

Khadijah bint Khuwaylid

Khadijah was the first wife of the Prophet Muhammad. She was the first to listen to the Quran as recited by the Prophet and to accept Islam. She was a widow and a successful merchant belonging to the Asad clan. Before marriage, Prophet used to work for her and she was very impressed with him. She was 40 years old and he was 25 years old when they got married. They had a very happy and successful marriage which lasted for 25 years until she died. They had two sons and four daughters (the sons died in their infancy). Khadijah was the Prophet's closest companion and his greatest supporter. When the Prophet Muhammad told her about the first divine revelation from the Angel Jibril (Gabriel), he was scared and unsure. She took him to her cousin Waraqah, who told him that he was really a Prophet of Allah like the Prophets Musa and Isa. She supported and encouraged him in later years also when the Quraysh's cruelty to him and his followers increased. She gave every possible support to him and his

mission. She supported him when the rest of the world rejected him.

She died in 619 A.D., a victim of the food shortages created by the Quraysh's boycott of the Prophet, his family and his followers. She was the best of women and the best of wives. She was very dear to the Prophet Muhammad and he always missed and remembered her.

▶ **Moral:** In a marriage, a man and a woman should be companions. They should support and encourage each other in both good and bad times.

▶ **Key events:** Marriage to the Prophet Mohammad, the Prophet's divine revelation, the first to listen to the Quran and to accept Islam.

▶ **See the Quran:** *Al-Ahzab* 33:28; *Al-Kawthar* 108:3.

▶ **See in this book:** Muhammad and Ummahat al-Muminin.

▶ **Relatives:**

Husband	-	the Prophet Muhammad
Sons	-	Al-Qasim
	-	Abdullah
Daughters	-	Zaynab
	-	Ruqaiyyah
	-	Umm Kulthum
	-	Fatimah

▶ **Study Question**: How was Khadijah a perfect wife to the Prophet Muhammad?

Khawla bint Thalaba

Khawla bint Thalaba was the wife of Aws ibn As-Samit, a Madinan Muslim, during the time of the Prophet Muhammad. She was divorced by her husband through *zihar*, an old pagan custom of divorcing one's wife by simply saying: 'Be to me as my mother's back.' This custom was very insulting to women. It freed the husband of all his duties towards his wife and children and made it impossible for women to remarry. Khawla was in a helpless condition, having no one to support her and her little children. She went to the Prophet with her complaint. Thereupon, *Surah* 58, *Al-Mujadilah* (She Who Pleaded) was revealed. Her just complaint was accepted and this unjust custom was abolished. Certain new conditions and laws were introduced to protect the rights of the wife, especially from cruel and unjustified divorce.

▶ **Moral**: No human customs and laws can disregard and ignore the just rights of all creatures of Allah, especially the weak.

▶ **Key Events**: Divorce by *zihar*; revelation of *Surah* 58 *Al-Mujadilah*.

▶ **See the Quran**: *Al-Mujadilah* 58:1-5.

▶ **Relatives**:

Husband: Aws ibn as-Samit

▶ **Study Question**: What was *zihar*?

What was Khawla bint Thalaba's complaint?

What did *Surah* 58 reveal?

Al-Khidr

Al-Khidr (the green one) is described in the Quran as one of Allah's servants who was gifted with His mercy and knowledge. Due to these gifts from Allah he could understand the secrets of life and, therefore, could also bring about changes in the affairs of the world.

The Prophet Musa (Moses) was asked by Allah to travel to the union of the seas and to meet Al-Khidr, so that he could share some knowledge with the Prophet Musa. The union of the two seas is where the two arms of the Red Sea—the Gulf of Aqaba and the Gulf of Suez—join together. The Prophet, therefore, set out on this journey with his young disciple, Yusha bin Nun (Joshua). Al-Khidr had his doubts about taking the Prophet Musa with him, but allowed him to accompany on the condition that he would ask no questions about anything and be patient until he himself mentioned it. The Prophet Musa had faith; he adopted the true attitude of a learner and promised to obey with the help of Allah.

They both started their journey and boarded a ship. Al-Khidr bored a hole in the bottom of that ship. Then he killed a young boy. Finally they reached a city whose people did not welcome them. There Al-Khidr found a wall on the point of falling down, which he repaired without even asking for payment. The Prophet Musa was shocked, confused and full of questions. Then Al-Khidr explained to him. He bored a hole in the ship because it belonged to self-respecting poor people and the king's men were taking away everyone's ships to use

in the war. Due to this hole they did not take the ship and the poor people did not lose their only source of income and were not reduced to begging. The young man whom he killed was wicked and dangerous to his pious parents and also to society. He took his life only after being authorized to do so by Allah, who had also promised another son who would be good to them. He repaired the wall, as it belonged to two orphans and there was treasure beneath it belonging to their righteous father. If it had fallen, their treasure would have been looted. Allah's wisdom is beyond human knowledge. What seems like loss is actually a gain, a cruelty may be a real mercy; returning good for evil may really be justice and not generosity. Man's limited knowledge and his inability to see into the future result in sadness over apparent tragedies. But a true believer would never lose heart at such losses, as he has faith in Allah whose plan always works for the good of human beings.

▶ **Moral**: Divine knowledge is unlimited. Constant effort is necessary to gain knowledge with time. One should try to have knowledge which is always in contact with life as it is actually lived.

▶ **Key Events**: Meeting Al-Khidr, journey full of events, reasons for the actions of Al-Khidr.

▶ **See the Quran**: *Al-Kahf* 18:60-82.

▶ **See in this book**: Musa and Yusha bin Nun.

▶ **Study Question**: What do you understand from the acts of Al-Khidr?

What are the attributes of a good learner?

Al-Lat, Al-Uzza and Manat

Al-Lat, Al-Uzza and Manat are the names of the three main goddesses worshipped by the pagan Arabs, before the establishment of Islam. They were called the daughters of God. Al-Lat was in human shape. Her shrine was at Taif. It was worshipped by the people of Makkah. Al-Uzza had its origin in a sacred tree. Its shrine was at Nakhla between Taif and Makkah. It was worshipped by the Quraysh and the Banu Kinana. Manat had its origin in white stone. Its shrine was in Mashlal, between Makkah and Madinah. The tribes of Al-Aws and Al-Khazraj and Khuzaa used to start their Hajj from this site. The Quran says that they are false goddesses, just names given by the tribal forefathers and that they had no power in them.

▶ **Moral**: Allah is the only one who should be worshipped. The true source of light is Allah, to whom everyone has to return.

▶ **See the Quran:** *An-Najm* 53:19-23.

▶ **See in this book:** Muhammad and Quraysh.

▶ **Study Question**: Who were Al-Lat, Al-Uzza and Manat?

Luqman

Surah 31 of the Quran is named after Luqman. The Quran calls him a wise man. He was an Arab who came from a poor background. He refused worldly power and a kingdom. He is supposed to have lived a long life. He is known by the title Muammar (the long lived). His knowledge was correct and practical.

He believed in Allah and asked his son not to worship anyone but Allah, who is all-knowing. He also asked him to be kind to his parents, regular in prayers, just, patient even in suffering, and not to be proud, but rather to be modest. Moral laws are based on man's own good and are of no benefit to Allah. When we obey Allah, we conform to our own nature as made by Allah. Therefore, Allah's will is best for us. If there is any conflict between duty to man and duty to Allah, it means that something is wrong with the human will, and we should obey Allah rather than man. The beginning of wisdom is when we start conforming to the will of Allah. This comes naturally from a true understanding of our relation with Allah. True wisdom is divine wisdom – the two cannot be separated. Luqman followed the golden mean of virtue which can be seen in every sign of nature. In all our thoughts and actions we should be moderate like other creations of Allah.

▶ **Moral**: Wise are those who truly believe in Allah and His Laws and live in accordance with His will. This way we live in accordance with our own nature as made by Allah.

▶ **Key Events**: Luqman's teachings.

▶ **See the Quran**: *Luqman* 31:13-19.

▶ **Study Question**: How is true wisdom also divine wisdom?

Lut

The Prophet Lut (Lot) was the nephew of the Prophet Ibrahim (Abraham). His father's name was Haran. He was the first and perhaps the only one to answer the call of his uncle. The Prophet Lut also accompanied the Prophet Ibrahim when he had to migrate from Ur in Iraq to Syria.

The Prophet Lut was blessed with knowledge and judgement. Allah asked him to go to the cities of Sodom and Gomorrah in the plains to the east of Jordan, near the Dead Sea (Bahr Lut or Lut's Sea). People in these cities shamelessly indulged in unnatural crimes. The Prophet Lut asked them to stop their sinful activities and crimes against their own selves and nature. He asked them to fear Allah and obey Him. But the people rejected the message of Allah. They did not believe in Allah or His punishment and asked the Prophet Lut to bring it down upon them.

They not only rejected Allah's message but committed unspeakable crimes openly in public, even in their assemblies. Instead of being ashamed of their hateful acts, they mocked the Prophet Lut and other righteous people. They even warned the Prophet Lut that he would be cast out if he continued to preach Allah's message.

One day, two angels in the shape of handsome young men came to test these people and to deliver justice and punishment. But the Prophet Lut's people attacked his house and asked him to hand over those handsome young men to them. He begged them to leave them alone. But they refused. He found himself helpless and prayed for Allah's support. The Angels then revealed their true identity and asked the Prophet Lut to go away before the morning, when punishment

would be meted out. He went away with his family and believers, with the exception of his wife, Halsaqa, who was not loyal to him and who sided with the wicked people. She had no faith in the mission either of her husband or of the angels who had come as his guests. The next day there was a violent storm with the showers of stones and great blasts of noise which destroyed both the cities of Sodom and Gomorrah for the crimes they had committed against their own nature.

The land on the east side of the Dead Sea where these cities were situated is covered with sulphureous salts which are deadly to animal and plant life. It serves as an example of the destruction that followed upon the sins of people.

▶ **Moral**: Every crime has its due punishment laid down in the decrees of Allah. Allah's Mercy and Justice go hand in hand in all human affairs. Faith has nothing to fear and wickedness has only to turn and repent to obtain Allah's Mercy.

▶ **Key Events**: Message of the Prophet Lut, visit of angels, destruction of the cities.

▶ **See the Quran**: *Al-Anfal* 6:86; *Al-Araf* 7:80-84; *Hud* 11:74-83; *Al-Hijr* 15:57-77; *Al-Anbiyaa* 21:74-75; *Ash Shuaraa* 26:160-175; *An-Naml* 27:54-58; *Al-Ankabut* 29:26, 28-35; *As-Saffat* 37:133-138; *Az-Zariyat* 51:31-37; *An-Najm* 53:53; *Al-Qamar* 54:33-39.

▶ **See in this book:** Ibrahim and Wife of Lut.

▶ **Relatives:**

Uncle	-	the Prophet Ibrahim
Father	-	Haran
Wife	-	Halsaqa
Daughters	-	Rith, Rariya (Rawaya)

▶ **Study Question:** Why did angels come to visit Prophet Lut?

Majus

The Majus (Magians, Zoroastrians) were the followers of an ancient religion. This religion was founded by Zoroaster in 1400 B.C. and reformed by Zardusht in the sixth century B.C. It was the national religion of Persia before the coming of Islam. They considered fire as the purest and the noblest element. They worshipped it as the symbol of God. Their sacred book is Zend Avesta. In India they are known as Parsis. The Majus are mentioned in the Quran along with the Muslims and the People of the Book, as being judged on the Day of Judgement.

▶ **Moral:** Everyone will be judged on the Day of Judgement.

▶ **See the Quran:** *Al-Hajj* 22:17.

▶ **See in this book:** Byzantines.

▶ **Study Question:** Who were the Majus?

Maryam

Maryam (Mary), the mother of Isa (Jesus Christ), was born into a family of priests in Jerusalem. Her parents, Imran (Amran) and Hannah (Anna, Anne), were pious people. Hannah had promised Allah that she would dedicate her child to His service. Maryam, who grew under Allah's protection, was a pure and devout child. The Prophet Zakariyya (Zacharias), her uncle, was her guardian in the temple.

One day the angels came to Maryam and told her that Allah had chosen her out of all the women of the world and purified her. She was destined to be the mother of the Prophet Isa. They said her son would be held in honour in this world and the Hereafter and would be nearest to Allah. They also said that he would speak to people in childhood and in maturity. Maryam went away to a forest in Bethlehem to give birth to Isa, the miracle child. She gave birth to him all alone.

When she returned to her people with the child, they abused and insulted her. The new-born child defended his mother and preached to an unbelieving crowd.

Maryam was an extraordinary woman as she gave birth to a son without the regular physical means. But this did not mean that she and her son were more than human beings. They were signs for people and miracles to all nations. Chastity was her special virtue. Maryam is an example for the believers of all times and she holds a special place above all womankind. She is even called 'Siddiqa'—the truthful.

▶ **Moral:** Maryam fought against evil with her chastity and with the miracle of the birth of the Prophet Isa. She put her trust in Allah and was duly rewarded.

▶ **Key events:** Birth of the Prophet Isa.

▶ **See the Quran:** *Aal-Imran* 3:35-37, 42-51; *An-Nisaa* 4:156; *Al-Maidah* 5:75,116-117; *Maryam* 19:16-33;   *Al-Anbiyaa* 21:91; *At-Tahrim* 66:12.

▶ **See in this book:** Hannah, Imran, Isa, Yahya and Zakariyya.

▶ **Relatives:**

Mother   -   Hannah

Father   -   Imran

Uncle   -   the Prophet Zakariyya

Aunt   -   Elisabeth

Son   -   the Prophet Isa

▶ **Study Question:** Why does Maryam hold a special place above all womankind?

Mikal

Mikal or Mikail (Michael) is one of the great angels of Allah. He is mentioned once in the Quran along with Jibril (Gabriel). He brings down the rain.

▶ **Moral:** Angels are given special powers and qualities to carry out their duties assigend by Allah.

▶ **See the Quran:** *Al-Baqarah* 2:98.

▶ **See this book:** Jibril.

▶ **Study Question:** What is the duty of the angel Mikal?

Al-Muhajirun

Al-Muhajirun (the migrants) were the early Makkan Muslims who went to Madinah leaving their homes and property behind to assist the Prophet Muhammad in his mission.

The first migration took place in 615 A.D., when the Quraysh started torturing the small Muslim community in Makkah. They went to Abyssinia. They were eleven men and four women, followed by a hundred more. Later they joined the Prophet in Madinah.

In 623 A.D. the Quraysh chief decided to assassinate the Prophet to stop the spread of the message of Islam. Allah revealed their plan to the Prophet. He then left for Madinah along with his friend, Abu Bakr. In all, 300 migrants followed him. They were taken care of by the Ansars (Helpers), the Muslims of Madinah. In this way, the brotherhood of Islam was established.

▶ **Moral**: The ties of belief are stronger than any other ties.

▶ **Key Events**: Hijrah.

▶ **See the Quran**: *At-Tawba* 9:100; *Al-Hashr* 59:8-9; *Al-Munafiqun* 63:7.

▶ **See in this book:** Al-Ansar, Muhammad and Sahaba.

▶ **Study Question**: Who were Al-Muhajirun?

Why did they leave Makkah?

Who helped them in Madinah?

Muhammad

Every Prophet was sent to a particular people with a specific mission to fulfill. They dealt with one aspect of life. But the Prophet Muhammad was sent to all mankind with the issues of life and death, the message of Allah, the One Universal God. In his mission and life, he dealt with all the aspects of life which different prophets in different places and times had dealt with. There is a final revelation in the Quran which confirms the previous scriptures, corrects the errors which men introduced into them and explains many points in detail for all those who seek right worship of and service to Allah.

The Prophet Muhammad was born on 22nd April 570 A.D. in Makkah, to Abdullah ibn Abd Al-Muttalib and Aminah. His father

died two months before his birth and his mother died when he was six years old. His grandfather, Abd Al-Muttalib, took care of him and after his death, when the Prophet Muhammad was eight years old, his uncle, Abu Talib, brought him up with his own family. His grandfather was the head of the Quraysh tribe, the guardian of the Ka'bah and protector of the pilgrims who visited this holy place. The Prophet Muhammad always used to be by his grandfather's side in all important meetings and discussions. He was a very thoughtful boy. He took good care of his family's sheep. He spent much time wondering about the mysteries of Nature. Even as a young boy he believed in one God, the God of the Prophet Ibrahim (Abraham). As he grew older, he became known for his righteousness, tolerance, patience, truthfulness and trustworthiness. His sense of justice and concern for fellow men made him a leader among his men. His experience of trading and honesty attracted the attention of Khadijah, a 40 year old widow and a rich merchant. She employed him to take her goods to trade in Syria. She was impressed with him and offered herself to him in marriage. He was 25 years old. They had a happy and a comfortable marriage. They had six children, four daughters and two sons. The sons died in infancy.

After his marriage, the Prophet Muhammad did not try to gain a position by mixing with the nobles of Makkah or enjoy his rich and comfortable life, but started wandering in the hills of the desert. He would often sit in the cave of Hira near the top of Jabal an-Nur, which was three miles away from Makkah. He would pray, look for the truth and seek answers from Allah to his questions. Finally on 12th February 610 A.D. in the month of Ramadan the Prophet's quest was rewarded. Allah sent the Angel Jibril (Gabriel) to him in the shape of a human being who taught him the words which appear at the beginning of Surah 96 *Iqra* of the Quran. He kept receiving these revelations for the next 23 years, through the Angel Jibril. In the beginning, the Prophet was very scared and couldn't believe that he was Allah's prophet. Khadijah comforted him and took him to her cousin, Waraqah, who told him that he was indeed Allah's messenger, just like the Prophet Musa and the Prophet Isa. Khadijah was the first to become a Muslim, followed by Ali, his cousin, and Zayd, his foster son. The first person to convert from outside the family was Abu Bakr,

a respected merchant, who became the Prophet's closest companion.

The Quraysh did not like the spread of the Prophet Muhammad's message of the one God; of protecting the weak, of the equality of mankind—rich or poor, man or woman and of the equal distribution of wealth. The Quraysh was a rich tribe which earned a great deal from the worship at the Ka'bah. They were also very proud and did not want to progress and change the ways which were followed by their forefathers. The Prophet's message reduced their power over people and also their income. The Quraysh did not like the message. It went against their interests. To stop the Prophet from spreading his message, they started using force on him, his family and his followers. The Quraysh even imposed a boycott on the small Muslim community, which prevented them from having any dealings with others. The women and children had to eat leaves for food. Unable to bear the hardships, some Muslims, on the advice of the Prophet, migrated to Abyssinia (Ethiopia) in 615 A.D. where a kind Christian ruler, king Najashi (Negus), gave them shelter.

Due to these hardships, Khadijah's health suffered and she died in 619 A.D. In the same year Abu Talib, his loving uncle and guardian, also died. The Prophet felt very lonely without them. Meanwhile the Quraysh's cruelty to the Muslims increased. The Prophet went to Taif, a city near Makkah, to spread Allah's message and sought help, but the people refused to listen to him. They insulted him, drove him out of the town and threw stones at him, making him bleed from head to toe. At this point, when he was very low, he had an extraordinary experience – Al-Isra and Al-Miraj (the night journey from Jerusalem to the seventh heaven and the Ascension). It was the turning point from which he took comfort and gained the strength to go on. It convinced him that Allah was with him.

The Prophet started preaching to pilgrims and travellers who came to Makkah. They were mainly from Madinah. The Quraysh chiefs at this point decided to secretly kill the Prophet. When the Prophet came to know about the conspiracy, he migrated to Madinah with Abu Bakr, where Islam already started to spread. On the way they hid in the cave of Thawr for three nights. The Prophet reached Madinah in 622 A.D., where he was welcomed by the people with great joy. All those who had migrated with the Prophet—the Muhajirun— were treated as brothers and sisters by the Muslims of Madinah, the Ansar. A brotherhood was formed—bound not by blood but by shared beliefs. The Prophet founded the mosque which is now known as Al-Masjid an-Nabawi, or the Prophet's Mosque. It became the centre of his activities by which he would promote the growth of Islam.

The Prophet's migration to Madinah angered the Quraysh, as they saw that the Muslims were becoming stronger. Only two years after the Prophet's migration, a one thousand strong Quraysh army came to fight the Muslims. The battle took place at Badr, a group of wells, about eighty miles from Madinah. The Prophet led a group of just 313 men, with two horses and seventy camels. Allah helped the Muslims to defeat the proud Quraysh army. This defeat angered the Quraysh and their allies, therefore, a number of other battles—Uhud, the Trench, Khaibar and Hunain took place in the space of the next

few years. The Muslims faced difficult times; they even lost the battle of Uhud. But after the battle of Hunain, Islam became the established religion of Arabia.

In the sixth year of the Hijrah, or 628 A.D., the Prophet set out for Makkah with 1400 companions to perform the Umrah. But the Quraysh stopped them about 11 kilometers from Makkah at Al-Hudaybiyya. Here the Prophet signed a treaty with the Quraysh, accepting almost all their demands. The Muslims returned without performing Umrah but they had made peace and a ten year no-war pact. In the next two years, the number of the Muslims increased from 1500 to 10,000. After some time, the Quraysh started breaking the peace treaty of Al-Hudaybiyya by secretly supplying weapons to other enemies of the Muslims. So in the eighth year of the Hijrah or 630 A.D., the Prophet along with a band of ten thousand supporters went to Makkah. The purpose was not to go to war but to scare the proud Quraysh into submission. The Prophet was proved right – the Muslims conquered Makkah without any bloodshed. In spite of such a great victory, the Prophet remained humble and forgiving. He walked through the city with his head bowed and did not kill or punish his enemies. He cleaned and purified the Ka'bah of all the pagan idols and Bilal ibn Rabah, in his strong and beautiful voice, called (*adhan*) the faithful to prayer.

The Prophet returned to Madinah and the Quraysh became Muslims. One by one, the rest of the tribes in Arabia entered the fold

of Islam. In 632 A.D., in the tenth year of Hijrah, the Prophet went on his last Hajj, commonly known as *Hajjat at-Wida* (The Farewell Hajj). This time 100,000 believers accompanied him. Here the Prophet gave his famous final speech, *Khutba* of the *Hajjat al-Wida*, at Arafat. The last *Surah Al-Maidah* 5:4-5, of the Quran was revealed to him. 'Today I have perfected your religion and I have completed My blessing upon you, and I have approved Islam for your religion'. After the speech he cried to Allah to tell him whether he had been able to fulfill his mission, then he asked the gathering the same question. They said that he had fulfilled his mission.

The Prophet Muhammad died on 8th June 632 A.D. The people refused to believe that he had died. But Abu Bakr was able to calm the people by saying: 'O people! For those who worshipped

Muhammad, Muhammad is dead. But whosoever worshipped Allah, let him know that Allah is alive, and will never die.' The Prophet lived a simple and ordinary life. He lived his life as he preached. He remained a patient and grateful servant of Allah and brought the message of peace and truth to all mankind.

▶ Moral: The life of the Prophet Muhammad is an example for all mankind on how life should be lived, irrespective of nations or times. He is an embodiment of all Islamic teachings. He is a perfect role model.

▶ Key Events: Beginning of revelations, cruelty of the Quraysh, Hijrah, spread of Islam, the Prophet Muhammad's death.

▶ See the Quran: *Al-Baqarah* 2:104; *Aal-Imran* 3:144,159,164; *An-Nisaa* 4:46,70-71,170; *Al-Maidah* 5:4-5, 19; *Al-An'am* 6:107; *Al-A'raf* 7:156-158,184,188; *At-Tauba* or *Baraat* 9:61,128; *Yunus* 10: 2, 15-16; *Hud* 11:2-4, 12-14; *Yusuf* 12:108; *Al-Ra'd* 13:43; *Al-Hijr* 15:89, 97; *An-Nahl* 16:125-128; *Al-Kahf* 18:6,110; Al-Anbiyaa 21:107; *Al-Furqan* 25:30, 41-42, 57; *An-Naml* 27:91-93; *Al-Qasas* 28:46-47; *Al-Ankabut* 29:52; *Ar-Rum* 30:30; *Al-Ahzab* 33:6, 21, 28-34, 40, 45-48, 50-53, 55, 59; *Saba* 34:7-8, 28, 46-50; *Ya-Sin* 36:6; *Sad* 38:86; *Ash-Shura* 42:23, 48; *Al-Ahqaf* 46:8-10; *Muhammad* 47; *Al-Fat-h* 48:8-10, 18, 29; *At-Tur* 52:29-34; *An-Najm* 53:2-18, 56-62; *Al-Mujadila* 58:20-22; *As-Saff* 61:6, 9; *Al-Jumu'a* 62:2; *At-Talaq* 65:11; *At-Tahrim* 66:1,3-6,9; *Al-Qalam* 68:2,4; *Al-Haqqa* 69:40-43; *Al-Jinn* 72:20-23, 27-28; *Al-Muzzammil* 73:1-8,20, *Al-Muddaththir* 74:1-7; *Al-Insan* 76:24-26;

Abasa 80:1-10; *At-Takwir* 81:22-25; *Al-Alaq* 96:19; *Al-Baiyina* 98:2.

▶ **See in this book:** Abu Bakr, Ahl al-Bayt, Aishah, Ali ibn Abu Talib, Al-Ansar, Al-Muhajirun, Khadijah, Sahabah and Ummahat al-Muminin.

▶ **Relatives**:

Father	-	Abdullah ibn Abd Al-Muttalib
Mother	-	Aminah
Grand father	-	Abd Al-Muttalib
The First Wife*	-	Khadijah
Uncle	-	Abu Talib
Daughters	-	Zaynab, Ruqaiyyah, Umm Kulthum, Fatimah.

▶ **Study Question**: How was the Prophet Muhammad's mission different from that of the earlier prophets?

Describe the Prophet Muhammad's childhood.

Who brought Allah's revelations to the Prophet Muhammad and for how many years?

What are the names of the earlier Muslims?

What sort of hardships did the Prophet and his followers suffer?

What is the significance of the peace treaty of Al-Hudaybiyya?

---

*The Prophet Muhammad married other women after the death of Khadijah, the prominent among them was Aishah.

What did the Prophet say in his last speech?

How did Abu Bakr console people after the Prophet Muhammad's death?

Al-Munafiqun

When the Prophet Muhammad migrated to Madinah along with the other Muslims, the whole city of Madinah accepted Islam. But a few of them accepted Islam out of fear of the majority. They were hypocrites who did not have the courage to oppose Islam. They pretended to be Muslims, but they were actually unbelievers. They were called *Al-Munafiqun* (the Hypocrites). *Surah* 63 of the Quran is named after them. They appeared to be very nice and friendly and tried to be close to everyone.

They sometimes even worked for the cause of Islam to hide what was in their hearts. But they always secretly plotted against Islam and helped its enemies. During the crucial times of wars they spread rumours that the Muslims were losing and then left the battlefield on the pretext that they had to defend their homes and families. This was one of the reasons why the Muslims lost the battle of Uhud. Abdullah ibn Ubayy turned back with his 300 men, when he was half-way to the battlefield. The battle of Uhud showed the true mindset of the *Al-Munafiqun*; their oaths of loyalty to the Prophet Muhammad were all false. They even spread lies about the Prophet and his family members. They did what was evil and set up obstacles in the path of righteousness. In character they were unstable and could not be relied upon. They were not blessed with the Grace and Mercy of Allah and would surely go to hell. The Quran even asked the Prophet not to pray for them. They would never be forgiven. But those who

themselves sincerely asked for pardon and were willing to change themselves would be forgiven and protected from evil.

▶ **Moral**: The Hypocrites are a source of weakness in any society and are a danger to its health and its very existence. They appear to be decent, good men but are actually sinners.

▶ **Key Events**: Hijrah by the Prophet Muhammad, battle of Uhud.

▶ **See the Quran**: *Aal-Imran* 3:66, 167; *An-Nisaa* 4:142, 145-146; *At-Tawba* 9:53, 58, 64, 67, 68, 78, 80, 84, 124; *Al-Ahzab* 33:13, 61; *Al-Hashr* 59:11; *Al-Munafiqun* 63:1-2, 4, 7.

▶ **See in this book**: Abdullah ibn Ubayy, Aishah, Al-Ansar, Al-Muhajirun, Muhammad and Quraysh.

▶ **Study Question**: Who were the *Al-Munafiqun* and how did they harm the interests of the Muslims?

Musa

The Prophet Musa (Moses) was chosen by Allah to help his people (the Children of Israel) and to free them from the cruelty of Firawn (Pharaoh) and of the Egyptians. A hundred years earlier the Prophet Yusuf (Joseph) had made his father the Prophet Yaqub (Jacob) and brothers settle down in Egypt. The Children of Israel were their descendants. The Egyptians hated them, as they were not their own people and, therefore, treated them like slaves.

The year when the Prophet Musa was born to Yukabid and Imran, Firawn had ordered that all the new-born boys of the Children of Israel were to be killed. Only girls were to be spared. He gave this order because a soothsayer had informed him that a boy would be born that year among the Children of Israel who would destroy his kingdom. But the Egyptian's cunning and wickedness were no match for Allah's plan for those who had faith in Him. Yukabid hid her son for three months but, when she couldn't hide him any longer, she put him in a box and left it floating down the River Nile. The box was picked up by a member of Firawn's household and brought to Queen Asiyah. She was a kind lady. She begged Firawn to adopt him as a son. Thus the Prophet Musa was brought up by the enemies of his people. But by the Grace of Allah he remained throughout in touch with his real family also. As a child he refused to take milk from the nurses. The Prophet Musa's sister who had followed him suggested to the Queen that she engage her mother as his wet nurse. In this way Allah restored him to his mother also. He was then raised to learn the knowledge of the Egyptians and to preach Allah's truth to them as one who had been brought up among themselves; he also strove to unite and save his own people and eventually led them to a new world and religion.

One day when he was grown up, he accidentally killed an Egyptian in order to save a man of the Children of Israel. He became very worried and asked for Allah's forgiveness. When he came to know that Firawn was enraged and had decided to kill him, he left Egypt. Finally he reached Madyan. There he helped two sisters by drawing

water from a well for their animals. They were very pleased at this act and took him to their father. The Prophet Musa told him the truth. He was impressed and offered his daughter, Safura (Zipporah), in marriage to the Prophet Musa. He married her and stayed for about eight to ten years with them. When he set out with his family he saw fire on the mountain of Tur and went towards it to bring back a burning brand from it. When he reached there, he heard a voice from above the trees on the right side of the sacred valley. Allah talked to him and blessed him with the ability to perform miracles and the supreme revelation. Allah asked him to go to Firawn and his people and to preach them the oneness of God and the glory of righteousness. The Prophet Musa prayed to Allah to cure his stammer and give him his brother, the Prophet Harun (Aaron), to assist him. Allah granted his prayer and asked him not to fear as He was with them.

Charged with this divine mission, the Prophet Musa reached Egypt. But the people rejected him and his brother and called their signs cheap magic. The Egyptians accused the Prophet Musa of plotting to deprive them of their land, and of parctising black magic. However, both charges were false. He only wanted to spread the message of Allah and free his people from the bondage of the Egyptians. They asked him first to approach Firawn and, if he agreed, they too would follow him. The Prophet Musa appealed to Firawn to give up his proud, cruel ways and bow before Allah. Firawn became furious and asked him to show the proof of his prophethood. The Prophet Musa threw his staff on the ground and it turned into a living serpent. He took his hand out of his armpit, and it shone a dazzling white. But Firawn and his people only called him a magician. They decided to call the best of their magicians to challenge his magic on the festival day.

Firawn in his pride was amused with Prophet Musa. The Prophets Musa and Harun were confident not about their own powers but about Allah and their mission. In the end, arrogance was humbled and humility and faith were protected and advanced. On the festival day Firawn's magicians threw down their ropes and sticks, which with magic tricks became serpents and climbed upon the Prophet Musa. When he threw his staff down, it turned into a huge serpent and swallowed all the other serpents. The magicians realised that this was not a magic trick, but a real sign from the Almighty, so they bowed and declared that they believed in Allah—the God of the Prophets Musa and Harun. The mission of the Prophets Musa and Harun was fulfilled. The magicians now turned their backs on their past lives of false worship and oppression of the weak. They now believed in the the one true God. Firawn become mad with rage and threatened to kill them cruelly. But they were not frightened by him, and instead asked for the forgiveness of Allah for their sins.

The Prophet Musa again warned Firawn and his people that, if they did not change their cruel ways and did not believe in Allah, they

would be punished. They did not listen and invited His punishment. They were struck by famines, floods, diseases and then the river water also turned red. After every punishment they begged the Prophet Musa to save them. But no sooner were they saved than they went back to their old, cruel, evil ways.

It is the duty of kings and leaders to show the right path to their followers. Firawn, on the contrary, led his people astray and became the cause of the destruction of his subjects. With the passage of time Firawn's cruelty increased towards the Prophets Musa, Harun and other believers. There was a reign of terror with no mercy shown to the Children of Israel. For this reason, many of the Prophet Musa's people left him, only a few remaining as his followers. But he did not become hopeless and remained steadfast in his faith. He continued to ask the Egyptions to believe in Allah, to stop their cruelty and to allow the Children of Israel to leave Egypt. Allah then asked him to take his people out of this cruel land. The Prophet Musa took his people with him and moved towards the deserts of Saina (Sinai). When they reached the banks of Red Sea they saw Firawn and his huge army following them. They were scared but the Prophet Musa's faith was unshaken. Allah asked him to strike the sea with his staff. The waves of the sea parted and the sea bed now exposed became a dry path. The Prophet Musa and the believers crossed over, but Firawn and his followers were drowned when they followed them.

The Children of Israel settled in the vast plain of Saina. There was scarcity of water and food, but Allah provided them with both. But

many of them were thankless and missed the variety of food of Egypt. The Prophet Musa was shocked at their ways and asked how they could miss Egypt where only slavery and cruelty awaited them.

After some time, the Prophet Musa was asked by Allah to go to Mount Saina to receive His revelations. Before leaving for the Mount for forty days he appointed his brother, the Prophet Harun, as the leader of the Children of Israel. But his people's faith in Allah was weak and they were impatient. On the advice of Samiri, they created a golden idol in the shape of a calf and started worshipping it. They did not listen to the Prophet Harun.

The Prophet Musa returned with the Ten Commandments and the Torah. They were directions and divine guidance for all people in all ages to lead their lives in accordance with a purpose and will of

Allah. The Prophet Musa could not control his anger on seeing that the Children of Israel were worshipping a golden calf. He was angry with his brother also, but then understood the Prophet Harun's helplessness and prayed to Allah for forgiveness and help. He knew it was a trial, in which some of his people had failed and, therefore, deserved punishment. He burnt the golden calf and punished the unbelievers.

Afterwards the Prophet Musa was ordered by Allah to lead the Children of Israel to the holy land (Palestine). The Children of Israel always questioned their Prophet and refused to enter the holy land because they were scared of the people living there. Except for a few, most of them did not trust Allah. As a punishment for not obeying Allah, they were made to wander homeless for 40 years. The Prophet

Musa prayed to Allah to let him die close to the holy land. He died when he was 120 years old, and was buried on a mountain near the holy land. Later the new generation, who had suffered the hardships of the wilderness, fought and defeated the cruel Amalekites who were ruling Palestine and Syria at that time and entered the holy land.

The Children of Israel had a double trial. In the suffering of bondage, they had learnt patience and constancy and, when they were freed, they learnt humility, justice and the righteousness of prosperity. The name of the Prophet Musa is the most often mentioned (130 times) in the Quran. Allah also talked to him directly.

▶ **Moral**: Laws based on any kind of hatred have to come to an end. One should not be cruel to people just because they are different. Those human beings who believe in Allah's truth when in a humble position but change their stance when in a better position are as bad as those who do not believe in Allah due to their arrogance.

▶ **Key Events**: Birth of the Prophet Musa, his bringing up in the household of Firawn, return to Egypt, leading the Banu Israil out of Egypt, bringing of the scriptures, the Banu Israil's worship of idols again, the refusal of the Children of Israel to enter the holy land.

▶ **See the Quran**: *Al-Baqarah* 2:51-61; *An-Nisaa* 4:164; *Al-Maidah* 5:23-29; *Al-An'am* 6:84; *Al-A'raf* 7:103-145,148-156,159-162; *Yunus* 10:75-92; *Hud* 11:96-99, 110; *Ibrahim* 14:5-8; *Al-Israa* 17:101-103; *Al-Kahf* 18:60-82; *Maryam* 19:51-53; *Ta-Ha* 20:9-80,

86-98; *Al-Muminun* 23:45-49; *Al-Furqan* 25:35-36; *Ash-Shuaraa* 26:10-69; *An-Naml* 27:7-14; *Al-Qasas* 28:4-42; *As-Saffat* 37:114-122; *Gafir* 40:23-46; *Az-Zukhruf* 43:45-56; *Az-Zariyat* 51:38-40; *An-Najm* 53:36; *As-Saff* 61:5; *At-Tahrim* 66:11; *An-Nazi'at* 79:15-26; *Al-A'la* 87:19.

▶ **See in this book:** Banu Israel, Firawn, Haman, Harun, Al-Khidr, Qarun, Safura, Sahara Firawn, As-Samiri, Shaman and Umm Musa.

▶ **Relatives:**

Father	-	Imran
Mother	-	Yukabid
Brother	-	Prophet Harun
Wife	-	Safura

▶ **Study Question:** How was the Prophet Musa brought up in the family of Firawn?

What was the message of the Prophet Musa?

What were the signs of Allah which the Prophet Musa was blessed with?

What did the Egyptians call these signs of Allah?

How did the Children of Israel escape from Egypt?

Namrud

Namrud (Nimrod) was the king who ruled ancient Iraq in the time of the Prophet Ibrahim (Abraham). It is said that his full name was Namrud ibn Kanan. He was worshipped as a god by his subjects. The Quran says that it was Namrud with whom the Prophet Ibrahim had disagreement. Namrud said that, like God, even he could give life or death. Then the Prophet challenged him to make the sun rise from west if he was a god. Namrud had no answer for this. The Prophet Ibrahim's message challenged the king's authority in his own country. So he became very angry with the Prophet Ibrahim, forcing him to leave for Syria.

- ▶ **Moral**: Sinners in their pride cannot see the truth and thus bring about their own destruction.

- ▶ **Key Events**: Message of Prophet Ibrahim, argument with Namrud, migration to Syria.

- ▶ **See the Quran:** *Al-Baqarah* 2:258.

- ▶ **See in this book:** Ibrahim.

- ▶ **Study Question**: What argument did the Prophet Ibrahim have with Namrud?

Naqib

Naqib means the leader. In the story of the Prophet Musa (Moses) in the Quran, twelve Naqibs (leaders) of the Children of Israel are mentioned. Each one of them was appointed to look after one of their tribes. Yusha bin Nun (Joshua) was one of them.

- ▶ **Moral**: A leader has power mainly to fulfill his responsibilities towards his people.

- ▶ **Key Events**: Appointment of leaders.

- ▶ **See the Quran:** *Al-Maidah* 5:12.

- ▶ **See in this book:** Al-Asbat, the Children of Israel, Musa and Yusha bin Nun.

- ▶ **Study Question**: How many Naqibs were there and what were their duties?

An-Nasara

An-Nasara is the term used for the Christians in the Quran. The Christians are also included among Ahl-al-Kitab (the People of the Book)—the followers of divinely revealed religions. The Quran says that the sincere Christians have the greatest affinity with the Muslims. They are also praised for their humility and devotion to learning.

▶ **Moral**: The Christians who are true to their religion can understand and appreciate Islamic virtues.

▶ **Key Events**: Messages of the Prophet Isa and the Prophet Muhammad.

▶ **See the Quran:** *Al-Maidah* 5:82.

▶ **See in this book:** Ahlat-Kitab, Ashab al-Ukhdud, Isa, Hawariyyun and Maryam.

▶ **Study Question**: What does the Quran say about the Christians?

Nasr

Nasr is the name of the idol worshipped during the time of the Prophet Nuh (Noah). The name of Nasr appears in the Quran along with the names of the other four idols: Wadd, Suwwa, Yaghuth and Yauq. Nasr was in the shape of an eagle, representing sharp sight. It is said that all these idols were the names of the righteous men of the people of the Prophet Nuh. After their death, people made statues of them to remember them by but later generations began to worship them as idols.

▶ **Morals**: Pagan beliefs do not add to human knowledge or human well-being. They only increase errors and wrongdoing.

▶ **Key Events**: Message of the Prophet Nuh.

▶ **See the Quran**: *Nuh* 71:23.

▶ **See in this book**: Nuh, Suwwa, Wadd, Yaguth and Yauq.

▶ **Study Question**: What were the names of the other four idols and who were they?

What did Nasr represent?

Nuh

The Prophet Nuh (Noah), a true messenger of Allah, is mentioned many times in the Quran. *Surah* 71 of the Quran is named after him. The Prophet Nuh's mission was one of guidance and mercy to warn

men against evil and to turn back to Allah. The Prophet Nuh's people were wicked and cruel to the poor and they had turned away from Allah's truth. They worshipped idols - Wadd, Suwa, Yaghuth, Yauq and Nasr.

Like a good messenger of Allah, he preached the message of Allah in public and in private to his people. He humbly informed them that he was a messenger of Allah. He asked them to seek pardon from Allah and to follow His path. He informed them about the Day of Judgement when everyone would be judged according to his or her deeds. But the wicked people did not believe him. They called him a liar and even a madman. They even beat him. Nevertheless, the Prophet Nuh urged them to believe him as he was one of their own and told them that he was not a liar and had no selfish desires of his own. He looked only to Allah for his reward. The rich people further insulted him for having only poor men as his followers. He gently and patiently continued reminding them of Allah, their Lord, and their ultimate return to His judgement seat. But they refused to listen to him. They even became angry with him and challenged him to bring disaster down upon them. The Prophet Nuh told them that only Allah could punish them and He would surely punish them if they did not give up their evil ways and seek His forgiveness. The Prophet Nuh then asked Allah for help in his mission. Allah told him that there could be no compromise with evil; there was no hope of saving the sinners, who were bringing about their own destruction. He told the Prophet Nuh that a great flood would destroy them and ordered him to construct a great and sturdy Ark (a ship), which would remain afloat in the floods. The Prophet Nuh warned his people about the approaching floods which would be their punishment. Instead of correcting their ways, they mocked him all the more.

When the Ark was ready, Allah asked him to take a male and a female of every living creature along with all the believers in it. Soon it started raining and water also started gushing out of the earth. The Prophet Nuh's son Kanan did not join him and, like other unbelievers, had more faith in material things than in Allah. He went up into the mountains to save himself, but the mountain-high waves drowned him. The wife of the Prophet Nuh was also drowned because she too was an unbeliever. All the wicked, unbelieving people were drowned for their sins. The flood lasted for fifteen days. The Prophet Nuh and his companions landed on Mount Judi which is in Turkey. They were all thankful to Allah. The Prophet Nuh prayed for himself, his family and all the believers in all ages and in all places and for the destruction of evil.

The Prophet Nuh lived for 950 years, out of which about 350 years were after the flood.

▸ **Moral**: This story, about a sign from Allah warns mankind about the deliverance of the righteous and the destruction of the wicked. The evil cannot win against Allah's plan. Evil has to be destroyed to stop the spread of its corruption.

▸ **Key Events**: The Prophet Nuh's message, the great flood, the saving of the believers.

▸ **See the Quran:** *Hud* 11:25-26, 29-32,41,43-46, 48; *Al-Israa* 17:3; *Al-Muminun* 23:24, 27-29; *Ash-Shuaraa* 26:107,116; *Al-Ankabut* 29:14; *Al-Haqqa* 69:12; *Nuh* 71:5-9, 23, 26-27.

▶ **See in this book**: Kanan, Nasr, Suwwa, Wadd, Wife of Nuh, Yaguth and Yauq.

▶ **Relatives**:　　Wife　　-　　Waliya

　　　　　　　　　　Son　　　-　　Kanan

▶ **Study Question**: What was the Prophet Nuh's message and how did he rescue the believers from the great flood?

Qarun

Qarun (Korah) belonged to the Children of Israel. He left his people and became a close associate of the cruel Firawn in Egypt. He was very rich. Qarun was so blinded by his own pride that he thought it was his own knowledge, skill and cleverness which had earned him his wealth. That was why he believed that he was superior to everyone else. He did not know that all the good things in his life came only from Allah. Human beings are too weak and dependent on Allah to achieve anything without His Grace and Blessings.

Qarun became a miser, forgot his responsibilities towards the rightful needs of his own, his family and friends. He refused to give charity. He spread many lies about the Prophets Musa and Harun. Due to his belief in his power and his arrogance, he even rebelled against the Prophet Musa. When he was in his glory, many people envied his wealth and thought how happy they would be if they were in his place. But wise men knew that the reward of Allah in the Hereafter was best.

The Prophet Musa prayed for Allah's help when Qarun's pride and cruelty crossed all limits. Allah then made the earth swallow him up along with his riches. Once he had been destroyed, the people who had admired his wealth saw the truth. They realized that there were other things which were more precious and desirable than wealth. One should always thank Allah whether he be rich or poor. Those who reject Allah and His laws do not prosper.

▶ **Moral**: We are not capable of achieving anything without Allah's help. Wealth given by Allah should be spent in charity, good works, His cause and for the rightful needs of this life.

▶ **Key Events**: Qarun's destruction.

▶ **See the Quran**: *Al Qasas* 28:76-83; *Al-Ankabut* 29:39.

▶ **See in this book:** The Children of Israel, Firawn, Haman, Musa, Sahara Firawn and Shaman.

▶ **Study Question**: What do we learn from the life of Qarun?

Quraysh

The Quraysh was the noblest tribe of Arabia, to which the Prophet Muhammad belonged. *Surah* 106 of the Quran is named after them. They were the descendants of the Prophet Ismail (Ishmael) and, therefore, lived near the Ka'bah, the central shrine of Arabia, as its custodians.

Makkah was located on an important trade route which gave them honour, money and power over other tribes. As a matter of Arab custom, no war could take place at the Ka'bah. This made them very secure. Therefore, they became very rich and prosperous. It was all because of Allah. But they did not believe in His message of unity and purity brought by the Prophet Muhammad. They put up stiff opposition to it. They did not agree to change the religion of their

forefathers, of which they were very proud. They told the Prophet that, if he stopped his mission, they would make him their king. But he did not agree. When they could not stop him, they started being cruel to him and to the small Muslim community. This forced the Prophet and the Muslims to migrate to Madinah. The Quran asks the Quraysh that how they would protect themselves from the punishment of Allah.

After the treaty of Al-Hudaybiyya, a number of people from the Quraysh accepted Islam. When Makkah was conquered, all of them gradually accepted Islam. Later they formed a great caliphate and preached the teachings of Islam beyond Arabia.

▶ **Moral**: Religion should not be used to acquire money and power.

▶ **Key Events**: Coming of Islam, migration of the Prophet, Hudaybiyya treaty, conquest of Makkah, becoming Muslims and preaching Islam.

▶ **See the Quran:** *Al-Qamar* 54:43-46, 51; *Quraysh* 106:1-4.

▶ **See in this book:** Sahabah, Muhammad, Al-Muhajirun and Al-Ansar.

▶ **Study Question**: Who were the Quraysh?

Why were they so prosperous?

Did they believe in the message of the Prophet Muhammad?

What did they do to stop the growth of Islam?

When did the Quraysh accept Islam?

Ar-Ruhban

Ar-Ruhban is the term used for the ancient Christian monks, who did not live a worldly life. They did not get married and lived only for the cause of Allah. They are mentioned in the Quran along with Al-Ahbar (Jewish scholars and Priests). The Prophet Muhammad praised them for their works, but did not agree with their belief in not getting married, because this was not in accordance with the will of Allah.

▶ **Moral**: We have to believe in Allah and follow His laws completely. It is a sin to make our own laws and preach them as if they were Allah's laws.

▶ **Key Events**: Message of the Prophet Isa, message of the Prophet Muhammad.

▶ **See in this book:** Ahl al-Kitab and An-Nasara.

▶ **Study Question**: How the Quran describes the ancient Christian monks?

Sabiun

Sabiun was the religious group which followed the Prophet Yahya (John the Baptist). They believed in one God and the Day of Judgement. They prayed facing towards the Ka'bah. The Quran mentions them along with the People of the Book and also call them

righteous. They lived in ancient Iraq. A tiny community still exists in Iraq which may be identified with them.

▶ **Moral**: All the prophets spread the message of the one true God; it was the followers who created differences.

▶ **Key Events**: Message of the Prophet Yahya.

▶ **See the Quran**: *Al-Baqarah* 2:62; *Al-Maidah* 5:69; *Al-Hajj* 22:17.

▶ **See in this book:** Ahl-al-Kitab and Yahya.

▶ **Study Question**: Who were the Sabiun?

Safura

Safura (Zipporah) is said to be the name of the wife of the Prophet Musa (Moses). Without mentioning her name, the Quran refers to her in the story of Musa, when he travelled to Madyan to save himself from the unjust society of Egypt and the anger of Firawn (Pharaoh). In Madyan he helped two sisters by drawing water from the well for their animals. One of them was called Safura. They were very pleased with his doing so and took him to their father. The Prophet Musa told him about his past. He was pleased and asked him to marry one of his daughters and work for him. The Prophet Musa married Safura. He stayed and worked for her father for about eight to ten years.

▶ **Moral**: Women can be of immense support and good companions to their husbands.

▶ **Key Events**: Migration of the Prophet Musa.

▶ **See the Quran**: *Al-Qasas* 28:23-28.

▶ **See in this book:** Musa.

▶ **Study Question**: How did the Prophet Musa marry Safura?

Sahabah

Sahabah is the term used for the companions of the Prophet Muhammad. They were the closest to the Prophet. They memorised the Quran, collected his teachings and transmitted the *hadith*. In general, this term is also used for anyone who believed in the Prophet's mission and had seen him at least once in his lifetime. The number of such believers is estimated at more than one hundred thousand.

The Quran does not use this term but refers rather to the Prophet's Companions. It mentions their faith, sincerity, sacrifices, belief in the Prophet's mission and their joining him in his divine mission. After the death of the Prophet, they continued to spread the message of Islam all over the world.

The Companions of the Prophet were chosen to carry out Allah's wish that Islam should spread. They were to avoid the easy, quick way of doing things and to be patient instead. They did not place their personal desires and choices above Allah's will. The Companions gave up everything without caring about any reward in this world. It was as a result of their efforts that Islam grew. The Quran calls them 'the true believers', who shall receive mercy in the Hereafter. It also asks all other believers to pray for them.

The Prophet Muhammad called them role models for believers in all times. The early companions who had to leave their homes and belongings were called Al-Muhajirun (the migrants). The other group, who helped the Prophet and the migrants, were referred to as Al-Ansar. Allah made them brothers and united their hearts.

▶ **Moral**: For a perfect follower, his mission is supreme. To achieve his mission he should happily sacrifice everything.

▶ **Key Events**: The Prophet Muhammad's mission, migration.

▶ **See the Quran**: *Aal-Imran* 3:102,110; *Al-Anfal* 8:63, 74-75; *At-Tawba* 9:100; *Az-Zumar* 39:10; *Al-Fath* 48:29; *Al-Hujurat* 49:10; *Al-Hashr* 59:10.

▶ **See in this book**: Abu-Bakr, Ali ibn abu Talib, Al-Ansar, Al-Muhajirun, Muhammad, Umar ibn al Khattab and Uthman ibn Affan.

▶ **Study Question**: Who are the Sahaba?

What does the Quran say about them?

Sahara Firawn

In Egypt, during the time of Firawn (Pharaoh) all citizens were forced to believe in a pagan religion and magic. Firawn was the supreme god. They were also made to worship many forces of nature as well as animals, heroes and other gods. Priests were forced to actively practice magic. When Allah sent the Prophet Musa to preach about the one true God, He gave him the ability to perform miracles. This was to show the people that the religion based on magic which they were practicing was false.

Sahara Firawn is the term used for the magicians of Firawn whom he summoned to defeat the Prophet Musa's miracles. These magicians and Firawn were so confident of defeating the Prophet Musa that they even discussed the rewards which the magicians would get in return. Firawn thought that after defeating the Prophet Musa in the contest, he would be able to control the people more firmly through his religion. Therefore, he organised the contest on the festival day so that many people could watch it. Firawn and the magicians were confident of their knowledge and power, but the Prophet Musa was confident of Allah's power and guidance.

On the day of the festival the Prophet Musa first asked the magicians to throw down their cords and staffs. They did so and hey turned into snakes. But when the Prophet Musa threw his staff down it turned into a huge serpent and swallowed up their snakes. In the presence of truth, trickery and magic must come to an evil end. The magicians could see that this was not a trick but a real sign from Allah, whose glorious light fell upon them. They immediately bowed down and said that they believed in Allah, the Lord of the worlds, the Lord of Musa and Harun. They asked for Allah's forgiveness for their sins and for their practice of magic which had been forced on them. This made Firawn mad with anger. To save his authority in front of his subjects, he accused the magicians of being the secret followers of the Prophets Musa and Harun. He warned them of severe punishment and even death. But they were scared of the punishment not of Firawn but of Allah. They were ready to suffer and die. Their only desire was to be forgiven by Allah. The light of the message of Allah made them strong and fearless of the worldly power of Firawn.

▶ **Moral**: Truth is most powerful and it gives strength to those who believe in it. Allah is merciful and forgiving. He can enlighten anyone, even sinners, and make them follow the straight path.

▶ **Key Events**: Message of the Prophet Musa, contest between the magicians and the Prophet Musa.

▶ **See the Quran**: *Al-A'raf* 7:113, 116; *Ta-Ha* 20:68-70, 72-73.

▶ **See in this book**: The Children of Israel, Firawn, Harun and Musa.

▶ **Study Question**: How did Firawn's magicians become believers? Why did Firawn become mad with anger?

Sahib al-Jannatayn

Sahib al-Jannatayn were the owners of the gardens. Of them one was rich and the other was poor. The rich man's name was Tamlikha and the poor man's name was Mutis.

The rich man had two big gardens which were full of fruits. He was proud of his wealth and family. He thought he would have them forever. He did not think that all the things he had were gifts from Allah, but believed rather that they were the result of his hard work and clever planning. He was proud and unjust and did not believe that the hour of Judgement would come, and even if it came, he thought, he would still receive the best things.

Mutis, the poor man, tried to correct him by reminding him that man was made of dust. He asked Tamlikha, to be grateful to Allah for His gifts and this would help him to enjoy them more. Mutis warned

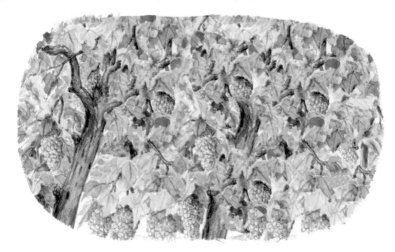

him about the short life of worldly goods. He said that though he was poor, he was blessed with Allah's guidance, which was most important.

The next day, the rich man's gardens were completely destroyed by a rainstorm. He realised his mistake and cried for forgiveness from Allah.

▶ **Moral**: Everything happens as decided and planned by Allah. Without Allah's help, no one can achieve a single thing on this earth.

▶ **Key Events**: Rich man's pride, destruction of his gardens.

▶ **See the Quran**: *Al-Kahf* 18:32-44.

▶ **Study Question**: Why were the gardens of the rich man destroyed?

Salih

Salih, a good man, who led a righteous life, was an Arab prophet sent by Allah to warn and guide his tribe, the Thamud. The Thamud lived in the north-west corner of Arabia between Madinah and Syria—a rocky land with fertile valleys and plains. They were great builders and agriculturists, and with their many skills they became rich. Their progress made them proud. Being idol-worshipper, they did not believe in Allah and His laws—or even in the Day of Judgement. They thought that they were not answerable for their deeds to anyone and felt very secure with their wealth and achievements.

The Prophet Salih asked them to stop worshipping idols and worship Allah instead, but they wanted to continue worshipping idols as their fathers did. They were also cruel to the poor and did not give them the rights to use water and common pastures. This made the Prophet Salih very unhappy, as he knew how wrong they were. He reminded them that all the things they had were only favours from Allah and that, they should, therefore, share them with everyone else. But the Thamud did not believe that he was a messenger of Allah and continued their evil ways. They even called him a foolish liar and gave no thought to his message. Once there was scarcity of water and the proud, rich people of Thamud tried to prevent the poor and their cattle from using the springs and the common pasture land. Allah asked the Prophet Salih to make his people understand that the water was to be divided between all of them and that each one had a right to drink water in turns. But the people did not listen to him. Even so, he

continued to ask his people to give up their selfish ways and let Allah's gifts on this free earth be available to all.

One day, to test his people, the Prophet Salih asked them to allow a she-camel (*naqat Allah*), which belonged to Allah to graze and drink. But they killed her and thus invited a grievous punishment. Instead of feeling sorry they planned to kill the Prophet Salih and his family. Their plot failed. Feeling very sad, the Prophet Salih still gave them three more days to think and mend their ways. But they did not mend their ways and only hastened their own punishment by their unjust ways.

A terrible earthquake buried them in their own fortress-like houses as if they had never lived there. The Prophet Salih and his humble followers were saved. The Prophet Salih felt bad that his people had not listened to him and sought Allah's forgiveness.

▶ **Moral:** The Thamud were rich and proud people who denied the poor their just rights by not sharing the gifts of Allah with everyone equally and, therefore, they were destroyed. Neither nations nor individuals, however mighty and prosperous or firmly established they may be, can survive if they disobey the laws of Allah.

▶ **Key Events:** Killing of she-camel, destruction of Thamud by a massive earthquake.

▶ **See the Quran:** *Al-A'raf* 7:73-79; *Hud* 11:61-68; *Ash-Shuaraa* 26:141-159; *An-Naml* 27:45-53; *Al-Ankabut* 29:38; *Fussilat* 41:13-14,17-18; *Az-Zariyat* 51:43-45; *Al-Qamar* 54:23-31; *Al-Haqqa* 69:4-8; *Al-Buruj* 85:17-20; *Al-Fajr* 89:9-14; *Ash-Shams* 91:11-15.

▶ **See in this book:** Ashab al-Hijr and Thamud.

▶ **Study Question:**

What were the people of Thamud proud of?

Why was the Prophet Salih unhappy?

As-Samiri

The Prophet Musa brought to the Children of Israel the message of the one true God. But in his absence, when he went to Mount Tur (Sinai) for forty days, As-Samiri (the Samaritan) made them lose sight of this ideal and he misled them into worshipping idols again. Saying that the Prophet Musa had forgotten his real god and also his people,

he helped them to make a golden calf from their ornaments and asked them to worship it.

When the Prophet Musa returned, he became angry seeing them worshipping the golden calf. Samiri started telling him lies. He tried to flatter the Prophet Musa and said that he saw in his footprints something sacred and supernatural. He threw some dust into the golden calf which made it utter lowing sounds. This made the Prophet Musa even angrier and he burnt the golden calf and cursed As-Samiri. It was due to him that a division in the followers of the Prophet Musa took place. Samiri was no doubt responsible for making the golden calf but the rest of the people were also responsible for following him.

▶ **Moral**: Everyone is responsible for his own acts and has to bear the burden of his sin.

▶ **Key Events**: Going away of the Prophet Musa, making of the golden calf, curse.

▶ **See the Quran**: *Ta-Ha* 20:85-97.

▶ **See in this book**: Children of Israel, Harun and Musa.

▶ **Study Question**: What did the Children of Israel do when the Prophet Musa was away for 40 days?

How was Samiri responsible for dividing the followers of the Prophet Musa?

Sarah

Sarah was the wife of the Prophet Ibrahim (Abraham). Without naming her, the Quran mentions her twice. The angels came with the good news to the Prophet Ibrahim that he was to have a son and his future generations would be a line of prophets. The Prophet Ibrahim and his wife, Sarah, had passed the child-bearing age. Sarah could not believe this news. She was informed that she would be the mother of Prophet Ishaq (Isaac), the grandmother of the Prophet Yaqub (Jacob) after which there would be a chain of prophets ending with the Prophet Isa (Jesus). Before the Prophet Ishaq, she had never given birth to any other child. Humanly speaking it seemed impossible that they could have a son at this age. Yet this is exactly what happened and this event became a cornerstone of sacred history.

▶ **Moral**: Anything can happen if Allah wills it.

▶ **Key Events**: News of the birth of Prophet Ishaq, birth of Prophet Ishaq.

▶ **See the Quran**: *Az –Zariyat* 51:29; *Hud* 11:71-72.

▶ **See in this book:** Ibrahim and Ishaq.

▶ **Relatives**:

Husband	-	the Prophet Ibrahim
Son	-	the Prophet Ishaq
Grandson	-	the Prophet Yaqub

▶ **Study Question**: What was the good news which Sarah received?

Shaman

Shaman was a secret believer in the message of Prophet Musa (Moses) in the Firawn (Pharaoh) household. In the Quran he is called 'the believing man' (*rajul mu'min*).

After the Prophet Musa had preached to Firawn and had a certain amount of success, Firawn and his people planned to take the life of Prophet Musa. At that moment Shaman tried to dissuade Firawn from killing the Prophet Musa. He argued that it was not correct to kill a man just because he believed in Allah, especially when he was of good character and behaviour. He said, moreover, that if the Prophet Musa was really a true messenger of Allah and had just come to tell them

the truth and warn them against evil, then Allah would surely punish them. Shaman asked them not to be arrogant because of their power. He appealed to them to refer to the past, to the way in which the generations of Prophet Nuh (Noah), the Ad, the Thamud and many more were destroyed for their sins. He also reminded them of the Day of Judgement when the wicked would be driven in to hell.

Some commentators even say that he might be the same person who earlier advised the Prophet Musa to leave Egypt after he had accidentally killed an Egyptian.

▶ **Moral:** The believers can see the true signs of Allah in His messengers.

▶ **Key Events:** Message of the Prophet Musa, plan to kill the Prophet Musa.

- ▶ **See the Quran:** *Al-Mumin* 40:28-40; *Al Qasas* 28:20.

- ▶ **See in this book:** Asiyah, Firawn and Musa.

- ▶ **Study Question:** What arguments did Shaman give to Firawn against killing the Prophet Musa?

Shamwil

Shamwil (Samuel) was the leader of the People of Israel in the 11th century B.C. This was about three hundred years after the death of the Prophet Musa (Moses). At that time the religious leaders used to be like dictators in their communities. They were called the Judges. In Shamwil's time, Israel suffered from corruption and attacks by the Philistines. The Israelites, instead of relying on faith and their own bravery, depended on sacred relics like the Ark of the Covenant, to help them in their fight.

At that time people insisted that Shamwil should appoint a king. They thought that a king would cure all their ills. But Shamwil knew that by asking for a king, they were just covering up their lack of faith and unity. However, he appointed Talut (Saul) as their king. They raised petty objections to this also.

- ▶ **Moral:** Believers should rely on their faith in Allah and their own capabilities.

- ▶ **Key Events:** Attacks of Philistines, appointment of Talut as the king.

▶ **See the Quran:** *Al-Baqarah* 2:246.

▶ **See in this book:** Children of Israel, Jalut and Talut.

▶ **Study Question:** What were the ills afflicting the Israelites at the time of Shamwil?

Shuayb

The Prophet Shuayb was an Arab who was sent to the people of Madyan and Ayka. Madyan was on the east side of the Gulf of Aqaba. It was on the important trade route linking Asia, Egypt and the Mesopotamian group comprising Assyria and Babylonia. The Midianites were initially followers of the Prophet Ibrahim but, over the next 500 years, they started adopting wrong practices in business and religion. They stopped believing in Allah and the Hereafter. They were commercially-minded people who engaged in dishonest business practices. They gave short measures and weights and did not give people what was rightfully due to them. They cheated people by means of all sorts of tricks in order to increase their profits. They also robbed travelling merchants passing along the highway.

The Prophet Shuayb reminded them of Allah's favours and also of the future of sinners like them. He said that he had a mission from Allah and he was not merely finding fault with them. He asked them to give up wrong ways of doing business because this would cut short

their prosperity in this world and also in the Hereafter. He gave them his own example of being poor, but yet being so happy and comfortable with what he rightfully deserved. He earned according to Allah's laws. He gave others their just dues and what he had left was not only enough but was the best possible provision for his own physical and spiritual growth.

The Prophet Shuayb told them that whatever advice he gave was for their own good. He did not ask them to do anything which he himself did not do. But his advice fell on hard hearts; it was easy to understand, but they refused to it. They denied that he was a prophet or that they were doing any wrong. They said they were good and tolerant people and they were doing what their fathers did. They asked the Prophet Shuayb and his followers to return to their old ways which were actually oppression of and cruelty towards the poor and the weak. His people first tried to bribe him and his followers. But neither bribes nor their appeals to be patriotic or venerate the ancestral religion moved the believers in Allah. The Prophet and his followers refused to practice their evil ways. Then the Midianites threatened the Prophet Shuayb and his followers with cruelty, insults and taking away their means of livelihood. They said that they could do all this as they were more powerful and richer than the believers. They warned the Prophet that they could easily imprison him and stone him to death, but they would not do so because of his tribe. But all their wicked designs rebounded on them.

The Prophet Shuayb again asked them to worship and fear Allah and to obey Him and His laws and believe in the Hereafter. They challenged him to bring down a piece of the sky if he had any real contact with Allah. But the Prophet Shuayb said that Allah was the best judge and only He would decide to punish them for their conduct. The Prophet Shuayb and his followers were ultimately forced to leave Madyan. But soon came a day of terror with showers of ashes which drove the Midianites into their houses. They were then punished by an earthquake. They were all destroyed as if they had never lived there. The Prophet Shuayb settled in Makkah, where he later died.

▶ **Moral**: Allah's laws should be followed in all aspects of life. One has to be just and fair and respect the rights of others while doing business.

▶ **Key events**: Message of Allah, destruction of the sinners.

▶ **See the Quran**: *Al-Araf* 7:85-93; *Hud* 11:84-95; *Ash-Shuaraa* 26:176-199; *Al-Ankabut* 29:36-37.

▶ **See in this book**: Ashab al-Ayka and Ashab Madyan.

▶ **Study Question**: Why were the people of the Prophet Shuayb punished by Allah?

Sulayman

The Prophet Sulayman (Solomon) was the youngest son of the Prophet Dawud (David). Like his father, he was a king who ruled Jerusalem and was also Allah's messenger. He was a very humble man and a firm believer in Allah's power. Allah gave him many blessings. He gave Sulayman power over the winds and the jinns—he could make them obey his orders. He had a knowledge of the birds, beasts, plants and insects, and could understand their language.

The Prophet Sulayman was just and wise. He had all kinds of desirable gifts from Allah. And with true gratitude he always thanked Allah for them. He did not use all these gifts in his own interests, but rather in spreading Allah's message and helping Allah's creatures. All his subjects, rich and poor, of different levels of intelligence, tastes and cultures were kept in due order by his discipline, justice and good governance, and they all gave him their co-operation.

He had been quite wise since his childhood. When he was only 11 years old, a farmer and a shepherd came to his father, the Prophet Dawud, to settle a dispute of theirs. Due to the carelessness of the shepherd, his sheep had entered a field and eaten and damaged the whole year's crops of the farmer. The Prophet Dawud asked the shepherd to give his sheep to the farmer to cover his loss. But little Sulayman gave a better suggestion, i.e. that the owner of the field should not take the sheep altogether, but only keep them till the cost of his actual damages was recovered from the milk, wool and possibly the lambs which would be born, and then return the sheep to the shepherd.

One day, when the Prophet Sulayman was passing through a valley with his huge army, he heard some ants asking each other to run home to save themselves because, by mistake, the army might step on them. Thanks to Allah's gift of understanding their language, he could take the necessary care not to kill the tiny creatures. The ever-humble Prophet Sulayman thanked Allah for His mercies which made him do right. He also pondered on Allah's greatness that how He took care of His tiniest creatures like the ants and protected them from a huge army.

His army consisted of men, jinns and birds. Once a hoopoe told him about Bilqis, the Queen of Saba (Sheba), who did not believe in Allah. He wrote to the Queen inviting her to accept the true faith. Instead of her submitting to the true religion, she sent gifts, which the Prophet Sulayman returned. Later, with the help of the worldly power, wisdom and patience which Allah had given him, he was able to convince her and made her and her subjects the true believers in Allah.

The Prophet Sulayman was fond of horses, but also loved the highest good. Once, while reviewing his horses he forgot to say his evening prayers. After he realised this, he became very upset with himself and asked for Allah's forgiveness.

When he was at the height of his power and glory, Allah tested him with a severe illness during which he was no more than a lifeless body on his throne. He realized how weak and powerless he was in the eyes of Allah. In his state of weakness and misery, he turned to Allah in humility.

The power, wealth and glory which were given to him were a trial for him. They might have tempted an ordinary man to descend into pride and evil. But the Prophet Sulayman always asked Allah for His forgiveness and guidance to use the power given to him to spread the light of Allah. All the gifts of Allah made him humbler. However great and glorious human power may be, it is temporary; it fades away even before people know of its decline. When the Prophet Sulayman was busy having a place of worship built by jinns, he died sitting on his throne, while leaning on his staff. No one realised he was dead until many days had passed, when a worm ate through his staff, and he fell down. Even the jinns could not make out that he was dead.

The Prophet Sulayman's earthly kingdom went to pieces after his death. But he would always be remembered for his righteousness, humbleness and being one of those who were nearest to Allah.

▶ **Moral**: Whatever one has is gift from Allah and should be used in righteousness and for the benefit of those around one. One should be humble and thankful to Allah.

▶ **Key Events**: Judgement of sheep, conversion of Bilqis, Queen of Saba, his death.

▶ **See the Quran**: *Al-Baqarah* 2:102; *Al-Anam* 6:84; *Al-Anbiyaa* 21:79-82; *An-Naml* 27:15-44; *Saba* 34:12-14; *Sad* 38:30-40.

▶ **See in this book**: Bilqis; Queen of Saba, Dawud and Ifrit.

▶ **Relatives**:

Father—the Prophet Dawud.

▶ **Study Question**: How did Allah test the Prophet Sulayman?

Why was the Prophet Sulayman's judgement better than that of his father, the Prophet Dawud?

What were the special gifts which the Prophet Sulayman had?

What did his army consist of?

How should the Prophet Sulayman be remembered?

Suwa

Suwa is the name of one of the pagan idols worshipped in the days of the Prophet Nuh (Noah). The other idols worshipped at that time were Nasr, Wadd, Yaguth and Yauq.

▶ **Moral**: It makes no sense to worship creations of Allah instead of Him.

▶ **Key Events**: Message of the Prophet Nuh.

▶ **See the Quran**: *Nuh* 71:23.

▶ **See in this book**: Nuh, Nasr, Wadd, Yaguth and Yauq.

▶ **Study Question**: Who was Suwa?

Talut

In about the 11th century B.C. there was unrest among the Children of Israel due to attacks by the Philistines, Amalekites, Amorites and other tribes. The people asked the Prophet Shamwil (Samuel) to appoint a king for them, under whom they would unite to fight against their enemies. The Prophet Shamwil knew this was just an excuse to hide their fear and lack of unity. Nevertheless, the Prophet Shamwil appointed Talut (Saul), a tall, handsome man from the small Binyamin (Benjamin) tribe. He was not a rich man, and the Children of Israil objected to his appointment as king. They said they had more authority and were richer than him. But the Prophet Shamwil replied that he would be their king, as Allah had chosen him and gifted him with knowledge. Allah grants his authority to whomever He pleases.

Talut set off with a large army to fight Jalut (Goliath), but it was not disciplined because many did not trust him. By means of a test

while crossing a river he got rid of all the doubtful men, who did not believe in Allah, and hence therefore were scared of Jalut and his warriors. But those who believed in the power of Allah and in the cause for which they were fighting marched ahead with Talut. Out of his original 80,000 strong force, he was left with just 300 soldiers. They prayed for Allah's help. Allah is with those who believe in Him and are patient. With Allah's help then, this small force defeated the mighty army of Jalut. The Prophet Dawud who also took part in this battle, killed the mighty Jalut thanks to his immense faith in Allah.

▶ **Moral**: In a war or a struggle, numbers do not mean much. The things which matter are the just cause, faith, determination, courage, discipline and the blessings of Allah.

▶ **Key Events**: War against Jalut and his army, killing of Jalut.

▶ **See the Quran**: *Al-Baqarah* 2:246-247, 249-251.

▶ **See in this book**: Dawud, Jalut and Shamwil.

▶ **Study Question**: Why was Talut appointed king?

Why did the Children of Israel object to Talut's becoming king?

Thamud

Thamud is the name of a tribe, frequently mentioned in the Quran, who were the descendants of the Ad. They were settled in a region of north-west Arabia, extending up to the north-east of Madinah, which is now called Madain Salih (the Towns of Salih). Their capital was situated at Petra, in what is now known as Jordan. The ruins of the Thamud's rock-dwellings can be seen to this day in Madain Salih. Their civilization shows traces of Egyptian, Syrian, Greek and Roman influences. They built fine temples, tombs and buildings cut out of the solid rock. They decorated them with sculptures of animals as well as many inscriptions. The Quran also calls them Ashab al-Hijr.

With the advance of material development, the Thamud people became godless. They started worshipping the goddess Al-Lat. They became proud and cruel to the poor. They did not share the gifts of Allah with the poor, even water and grasslands. Allah sent the Prophet Salih to guide them. But they refused to listen to him. He asked them

to allow the she-camel (naqat-Allah), a sign from Allah, to drink water. But they did not listen to him and killed her. Later the Thamud people were destroyed by an earthquake for their sins.

▶ **Moral**: However strong and advanced one becomes, if one does not follow Allah's laws, one will surely invite one's own destruction.

▶ **Key Events**: Message of the Prophet Salih, killing the she-camel, destruction of the Thamud.

▶ **See the Quran**: *Al-A'raf* 7:73-79; *Hud* 11:61-68; *Al-Furqan* 25:38; *Ash-Shuaraa* 26:141-159; *An-Naml* 27:45-53; *Al-Ankabut* 29:38; *Fussilat* 41:17; *Az-Zariyat* 51:43-45; *Al-Qamar* 54:23-31; *Al-Haqqa* 69:4-8; *Al-Buruj* 85:17-20; *Al-Fajr* 89:9-14; *Ash-Shams* 91:11-15.

▶ **See in this book:** Ashab al-Hijr and Salih.

▶ **Study Question**: Who were the Thamud?

Whose influence does their civilization show?

Thaqif

The Thaqif is one of the major tribes which are mentioned in the Quran. In 628 A.D, the Prophet Muhammad left Makkah for Taif with his family. He went there to give the message of Islam and to look for the support of the townspeople. The people of Taif belonged to the Thaqif tribe. They not only refused to support him but insulted him. They threw stones at him and badly injured him.

After the conquest of Makkah by the Muslims, the Thaqif and Hawazin tribes organised a major attack on the Muslims. Later, when the Thaqif had entered the fold of Islam, many great personalities emerged from amongst them. Muhammad ibn Qasim ath-Thaqafi, who brought Islam to the Indian subcontinent, was one of them.

▶ **Moral**: It is Allah's will whose heart He opens to the message of Islam and when.

▶ **Key Events**: The Prophet Muhammad's visit to Taif, the Thaqif's attack on the Muslims, their conversion to Islam.

▶ **See the Quran**: *Az-Zukhruf* 43:31.

▶ **See in this book**: Al-Asbat.

▶ **Study Question**: Who were the Thaqif?

Who brought Islam to the Indian subcontinent?

Tubba

The Quran mentions the people of Tubba twice. Tubba is understood to be a title or family name of the Himyar kings in Yemen of the Hamdan tribe. The Himyar were an ancient race. This title was given only to those kings of Yemen whose rule extended from Saba to Hadramawt and Himyar. The individual Tubba spoken of in the Quran was a believer, but his people were wrongdoers and hence were destroyed. Their earliest religion was Sabianism or the worship of the heavenly bodies. Later, at different times, they practiced Judaism and Christianity. The Prophet Muhammad sent out many envoys during 9-10 A.H. One such embassy was sent to the Himyar of Yemen, which led to their accepting Islam.

▶ Moral: A nation or people progresses from pagan religions to the true religion of Islam.

▶ Key Events: Envoys sent to invite people to accept Islam.

▶ See the Quran: *Ad-Dukhan* 44:37; *Qaf* 50:14.

▶ Study Question: Who were the people of the Tubba?

How and when did they accept Islam?

Umar ibn Al-Khattab

Umar ibn Al-Khattab was the second Caliph of Islam. He was one of the closest companions of the Prophet Muhammad. When he was a Caliph, Syria, Iraq, Egypt, Persia and Palestine entered the fold of Islam. He was the first to decide that the year of the Hijra should be the first year of the Islamic era. He was the first to receive the title of Amir al-Muminin (the Chief of the believers).

The son of Khattab ibn Nafayal, he belonged to the Adi tribe and shared his father's love of the old faith. He hated the Prophet Muhammad and was ready for violent action against him. Towards the end of 616 A.D., he decided to kill the Prophet Muhammad. In the meanwhile, he heard the news of the conversion to Islam of his own sister, Fatimah, and her husband, Said ibn Zayd. Enraged at this, he hurried towards their house. There he heard a part of the recitation of the Quran. He struck his sister and brother-in-law and demanded the leaf from which they had been reading. As he read the leaf, which had the beginning of *Surah Taha* 20, it touched his soul. He immediately went to the Prophet Muhammad and announced his change of faith.

Thereafter, he gave his entire life to the cause of Islam. His conversion was a big blow to the power of the Quraysh. He even started offering his prayers in public. Later he got his widowed daughter, Hafsah, married to the Prophet Muhammad. When the Prophet Muhammad died, it was with great difficulty that Abu Bakr consoled him.

He had the foresight of an intelligent leader. Once in Palestine, when he was sitting in the courtyard of the Church of the Resurrection in Jerusalem, the time of prayer came and the Patriarch of the Church suggested that he should pray in the church itself. But Umar refused as he felt that in future the Muslims would come and insist on making a mosque on the same spot where their Caliph had said his prayers. To avert the conflict that might arise in future, he offered his prayers some distance away from the Church. As he had foreseen, later the Muslims did make a mosque at the exact point where he prayed. It is known as Masjid Umar. He was also very kind and considerate. Once, during a famine, he passed an order to stop the cutting off of the hands of thieves.

He was killed in 644 A.D. by a Persian slave Abu Lulua Firoz, when he was leading worshippers in the mosque for dawn prayers.

▶ **Moral**: The words of Allah can soften the hearts of the hardest non-believers.

▶ **Key Events**: Message of the Prophet Muhammad, Umar's conversion, death of the Prophet, Umar's becoming the second Caliph.

▶ **See the Quran**: *Aal-Imran* 3:144; *Taha* 20:1-8.

▶ **See in this book**: Abu Bakr, Ali ibn Abi Talib, Muhammad, Sahabah and Uthman ibn Affan.

▶ **Relatives**:

Father	-	Khattab ibn Nufayl
Uncle	-	Abu Jahal
Son-in-law	-	the Prophet Muhammad
Daughter	-	Hafsah
Sister	-	Fatimah
Brother-in-law	-	Said ibn Zayd

▶ **Study Question**: How did Umar ibn al-Khattab accept Islam?

Why did not he pray inside the church?

What sort of a leader was he?

Umayya ibn Abi Salt

Umayya ibn Abi Salt was a hypocrite who lived during the time of the Prophet Muhammad. He refused to see the signs of Allah and turned away from Islam. It is said that in *Surah Al-Araf* 7:175-176, Umayya ibn Abi Salt is the person mentioned as turning away from the signs of Allah.

▶ **Moral**: To find the truth, one should have fear of God in his heart.

▶ **See the Quran**: *Al-Araf* 7:175-176.

▶ **See in this book**: Balam.

▶ **Study Question**: Who was Umayya ibn Abi Salt?

Umm Musa

Umm Musa, whose name was Yukabid bint Lawi was the mother of the Prophet Musa (Moses). Without naming her, the Quran mentions her in connection with the threat hanging over the Prophet Musa at the time of his birth. The Prophet Musa was born at a time when Firawn (Pharaoh) had ordered all new-born male children of the Children of Israel to be killed. But the Prophet Musa was saved by his mother, who nursed him for three months. When the danger of his discovery increased, Allah asked her to put her baby in a box and float him on the Nile. Allah promised her that her child would be saved and would

196

soon be restored to her. He revealed to her that her child would become His Prophet. The mother then had no cause to fear or to grieve.

▶ **Moral**: No human plan can succeed without the will of Allah. If Allah intends to save someone, no one can kill him.

▶ **Key Events**: Birth of the Prophet Musa.

▶ **See the Quran**: *Al-Qasas* 28:7.

▶ **See in this book**: Firawn, Harun and Musa.

▶ **Relatives**:
Son	-	The Prophet Musa
Son	-	The Prophet Harun
Husband	-	Imran

▶ **Study Question**: What did Allah promise the Prophet Musa's mother?

Ummahat al Muminin

Ummahat al-Muminin means the Mothers of the Believers. According to the Quran, the Prophet Muhammad's wives were the Mothers of the Believers. This shows the extent of the honour and respect they had in Islam. In the Quran, *Surah* 33 *Al-Ahzab* makes a special reference to the Prophet's wives. In this *Surah* they are given the option of remaining with the Prophet or separating from him, as his life was to be very tough.

This happened when they demanded some basic necessities for running of the home. In normal circumstances, such a demand on their part would have been quite in order, but in view of the historical role the wives of the Prophet were expected to play in his mission, their demands were not correct. Therefore, the Quran admonished them and asked the Prophet to give them the option of being separated from him. The Prophet Muhammad told them that he would not be able to give them normal worldly pleasures. They could not even afford to have simple meals. After the Hijrah (migration from Makkah to Madinah) he and his companions were in financial ruin, so the Prophet's wives were informed that they had no place in the sacred household if they wished for ease or worldly glitter. If such were the

case, they could be divorced and would be very well provided for. There was not much in the way of worldly goods or satisfaction that the Prophet could give them. But he was kind, just and true: the best of men to his family. They chose not to leave him and took an active part in his mission.

This *Surah* establishes the dignity and position of the Holy Prophet's wives who had a special mission and responsibility as Mothers of the Believers. They were not to be like ordinary women: they had to guide and instruct women in religious matters especially those who entered the fold of Islam. Islam is a way of life, and the Muslims are a family; women have an equal place in Islam with men, and their intimate instruction must be through women. Both men and women had spiritual as well as human rights and duties in an equal degree, and could look forward to the future reward of the Hereafter. They also visited and looked after those who were ill or in distress. During wars they would go with the other women to take care of the injured. They performed all the kindly offices which could assist the Prophet's mission.

Through their work they were expected to stand out as a sacred example, so that people would find them superior to themselves in character and morals. They were to make no vulgar worldly display, as was the custom in the times of paganism. Obedience to Allah's laws sums up all their duties along with regular prayers and charity. While they were to be kind and gentle to all, they were to be guarded on account of their special position, lest people might misunderstand or take advantage of their kindness. They were even asked not to appear informally without the veil except in front of the family. The screen was a special feature of honour for the Prophet's household, introduced about five or six years before his death. With their good deeds and sacrifices, they earned the position they had as Mothers of the Believers. The *Surah* also talks about the duties of the believers towards them. The Mothers of the Believers were to be treated kindly and gently and to be respected by the believers. No lies were to be spread about them.

The Prophet Muhammad's only marriage in his youth was with Khadijah who was 14 years his elder. She was his only wife for 25 years till she died. Later he had various marriages. Most of his marriages were with widows, not only to support them but also to set an example to other believers. Some of the marriages were done to prove various laws and teachings of Islam. The Prophet's wives

belonged to various tribes, clans and families. They became a connecting and a unifying link between their members. The marriages were part of his mission to spread Islam. He also needed them to help him in his duties of leadership. Even after the death of the Prophet, his widows continued to strive to spread the religion. The people continued to come to them to understand religion and also to be helped to make decisions in the light of religion. The Prophet's wives also helped in the compilation of the Quran and Shariah in Islamic teachings, and in recording the sayings and deeds of the Prophet. They helped in spreading Islam and the teachings of the Prophet to the Muslims and others for fifty years after his death, for almost two succeeding generations.

▶ **Moral**: In Islam, women and men are equal. They have equal social and human rights. The wives of the Prophet lived lives which set examples for all women.

▶ **Key Events**: The Prophet Muhammad's message, Hijrah.

▶ **See the Quran**: *Al-Ahzab* 33:6, 32, 34.

▶ **See in this book**: Aishah, Khadijah and Muhammad.

▶ **Study Question**: What was the role of the 'Mothers of Believers' in the mission of the Prophet Muhammad?

What was the duty of the believers to them?

Al-Ummiyun

Al-Ummiyun means the unlettered people. The Quran refers to Arabs by this name in *Surah Jumua* 62:2. It means the nation who had not earlier received any revealed scriptures of their own. The Quran also calls the Prophet Muhammad *'an-nabi al-ummi'*, the unlettered Prophet in *Surah Al-Araf* 7:157. This was to highlight the fact that he was not able to read or write, and was therefore, unable to derive his message from the previous scriptures as accused by his enemies.

▶ **Moral**: Allah's revelation is for the benefit of all men, whether they have worldly learning or not.

▶ **Key Events**: Revelation to the Prophet Muhammad.

▶ **See the Quran:** *Al-Araf* 7:157; *An-Nahl* 16:102-105; *Al-Furqan* 25:5; *Al-Jumua* 62:2.

▶ **See in this book:** Al-Arab and Children of Israel.

▶ **Study Question:** What does the Prophet being unlettered prove?

Uthman ibn Affan

Uthman ibn Affan was the third Caliph of Islam. He was one of the most devout companions of the Prophet Muhammad. He was a rich merchant of a noble family belonging to the Abd Shams tribe. He gave every possible support to the Prophet Muhammad and his mission.

Later he became related to the Prophet Muhammad when he asked for the hand of his daughter, Ruqaiyyah, and was married to her. In

the early days of Islam, when the cruelty of the Quraysh had become unbearable, the Prophet gave permission to the believers to migrate to other lands. Thus Uthman and his wife, Ruqaiyyah, migrated to Abyssinia. They stayed there for some time and then returned.

He played an important role in the spread of the Quran, making copies of it and sending them to many countries. The earliest copies of the Quran which still exist today are those made during his lifetime. They are named after him. Uthman is not mentioned in the Quran by name, but is called *as-sabiqun al-awwalun*, 'those who lead the way'. He was killed in Madinah in 656 A.D.

▶ **Moral**: Faith comes to people in various ways.

▶ **Key Events**: Message of the Prophet Muhammad, conversion to Islam, migration, becoming third Caliph of Islam.

▶ **See the Quran**: *At-Tawba* 9:100; *Al-Ankabut* 29:56.

▶ **See in this book**: Abu Bakr, Ali ibn Abu Talib, Al-Ansar, Muhammad, Sahabah and Umar ibn Al-Khattab.

▶ **Relatives**:
Father-in-law	-	the Prophet Muhammad
Mother-in-law	-	Khadijah
Wife	-	Ruqaiyyah

▶ **Study Question**: Who was Uthman ibn Affan?

How did he accept Islam?

Uzayr

Uzayr (Ezra) was a prophet who lived in the fifth century B.C. He was a scribe, priest and reformer who, after being released from captivity was sent by the Persian king to Jerusalem. There are many stories about him in the Jewish tradition. Some sects of the ancient Jews used to worship the Prophet Uzayr and called him the son of God. This is denounced in the Quran.

The Prophet Uzayr had a donkey on which he travelled far and wide. Once when he was passing through a ruined city he wondered how Allah would give life to this city, when it had been completely destroyed and was now dead. Immediately Allah struck him down dead along with his donkey. After a hundred years He brought him back to life. Allah asked him how long he had been away. He replied a

day or a part of a day. Allah then told him that he had been dead for a a hundred years. His food and drink were fresh. The donkey on which he was travelling had also died and only its bones were left. Before his very eyes Allah caused its bones to be reunited with its flesh and blood and thus restored it to life. The Prophet Uzayr was amazed. His belief in life after death was reaffirmed.

▶ **Moral**: Time is nothing to Allah. The key of life and death is in Allah's hands. There is life after death. Everyone will be raised on the Day of Judgement. Allah is All-powerful. Man's power is nothing without faith in Allah.

▶ **Key Events**: Passing through the ruined city, made to die, then restored to life.

▶ **See the Quran**: *Al-Baqarah* 2:259; *At-Tawba* 9:30.

▶ **Study Question**: What did the Prophet Uzayr think when he saw the ruined city?

What did Allah do to him and why?

Wadd

Wadd was the pagan idol worshipped, during the times of the Prophet Nuh (Noah). Wadd was in the form of a man representing masculine power. It is mentioned in the Quran along with four other idols: Suwa, Yaghuth, Yauq and Nasr.

- **Moral**: Only Allah should be worshipped, not His creations or qualities.

- **Key Events**: Message of the Prophet Nuh, destruction of sinners among the people of the Prophet Nuh.

- **See the Quran**: *Nuh* 71:23.

- **See in this book**: Nasr, Nuh, Suwa, Yaghuth and Yauq.

- **Study Question**: What was Wadd and what did it represent?

Al- Walid ibn Al-Mughira

Al-Walid ibn Al-Mughira was a chief of the Makhzum tribe. He was a wealthy pagan of Makkah and from the beginning was an enemy of the Prophet Muhammad. He abused and persecuted the Prophet and his companions. Al-Walid ibn Al-Mughira spread lies about the

Prophet and the Quran. He called the Quran magic, poetry and just a history. He is referred to in the Quran in many places, but not by his name. He came to an evil end just after the Battle of Badr.

▶ **Moral**: There have always been enemies of the truth. The rich and established people never welcome any change if it questions their power, even if it comes from Allah.

▶ **Key Events**: The Prophet Muhammad's message of Islam.

▶ **See the Quran**: *Al-Qalam* 68:10-16; *Al-Muddaththir* 74:18-25.

▶ **Study Question**: Who was Al-Walid ibn Al-Mughira?

What lies did he spread?

The Wife of Nuh

The name of the Prophet Nuh's wife was Waliya. The Quran does not mention her by name, but she is referred to along with the unbelieving wife of the Prophet Lut. Both women were married respectively to two of the great Prophets of Allah, but neither believed in her husband's message. No one becomes righteous by being close to the righteous. It is one's deeds which make one righteous. The husbands of these women could in no way protect them from Allah's punishment. The Prophet Nuh's wife, for example, died in the great flood along with all the other unbelievers. They were in great contrast to the wife of Firawn, Asiyah, who was a believer.

▶ **Moral**: Every individual is responsible for his or her acts. It is his deeds and actions that will earn him reward or punishment.

▶ **Key Events**: Message of the Prophet Nuh, great flood.

▶ **See the Quran:** *At-Tahrim* 66:10.

▶ **See in this book:** Nuh and Kanan.

▶ **Relatives**:

Husband	-	The Prophet Nuh
Son	-	Kanan

▶ **Study Question**: What makes a person righteous?

Wife of Lut

The Prophet Lut's (Lot) wife's name was Halsaqa. Without being named, she is mentioned many times in the Quran. She was disobedient to her husband. The world around her was wicked, and she sympathised with and followed that wicked world. She had no faith in Allah. When threatened with Allah's scourge, she stayed behind and shared the fate of the wicked inhabitants of the cities of the plain. One soul cannot lay claim to the merits of righteous souls just by being related or being close to them.

▶ **Moral**: Personal responsibility must be maintained before Allah. We are accountable for all our acts.

▶ **Key Events**: The Prophet Lut's message, destruction of the cities of the plains.

▶ **See the Quran**: *Hud* 11:81; *Ash-Shuaraa* 26:171; *As-Saffat* 37:135; *At-Tahrim* 66:10.

▶ **See in this book:** Lut, wife of Nuh.

▶ **Relatives:**   Husband   -   the Prophet Lut

▶ **Study Question**: What happened to the wife of the Prophet Lut? Why did it happen to her?

Yaghuth

Yaghuth was a pagan idol worshipped in the time of the Prophet Nuh (Noah) along with four other idols: Wadd, Suwa, Yauq and Nasr. Yaghuth was in the shape of a lion, representing strength.

▶ **Moral**: It makes no sense to worship creations of Allah.

▶ **Key Events**: Message of the Prophet Nuh, great flood.

▶ **See the Quran:** *Nuh* 71:23.

▶ **See in this book:** Nasr, Nuh, Suwa, Wadd, Yaguth and Yauq.

▶ **Study Question**: What was Yaguth and what did it represent?

Yahuda

Yahuda (Judah) was one of the ten stepbrothers of the Prophet Yusuf (Joseph). The Quran refers to him twice in the story of the Prophet Yusuf. When the other stepbrothers of the Prophet Yusuf decided to kill him, it was Yahuda who instead suggested leaving him in a dark well. Later when the Prophet Binyamin (Benjamin) was wrongly accused of stealing the king's cup and was asked to stay back in Egypt, Yahuda offered to stay instead of him.

▶ **Moral**: Weak people, even if they are good, can easily be encouraged to commit sins.

▶ **Key Events**: Leaving of the Prophet Yusuf, famine, visit to Egypt.

▶ **See the Quran:** *Yusuf* 12:10, 78.

▶ **See in this book:** Binyamin, Yaqub and Yusuf.

▶ **Relatives**:

Father	-	the Prophet Yaqub
Stepbrothers	-	the Prophet Yusuf
	-	the Prophet Binyamin

▶ **Study Question**: What is the role of Yahuda in the story of the Prophet Yusuf?

Yahya

The Prophet Yahya (John the Baptist) was the son of the Prophet Zakariyya (Zacharias). He was a cousin of the Prophet Isa (Jesus). His mother, Isha bint Faqudh, was the sister of Hannah (Anna, Anne), the mother of Maryam (Mary). While he was still quite young, he was given wisdom by Allah, for he boldly stood up against evil. He was kind to his parents and loved them dearly. He grew up to become a humble, gentle and straightforward person. He was a preacher of truth and led a life of solitude. In accordance with his father's prayer, he

and the Prophet Isa for whom he paved the way, renewed the message of Allah which had been corrupted and lost among the Israelites.

He was devout, and felt a gentle pity and love for all the creatures of Allah. He moved among the humble and lowly. He lived a pure life, having renounced the world and gone to live in the wilderness. He was granted prophethood at the age of thirty. According to the Quran his main mission was to pave the way for the Prophet Isa. He carried all his tasks in his youth. The Prophet Yahya did not live for long. He was imprisoned by King Herod, a provincial ruler under the Roman Empire whom he reproved for his sins. Later he was beheaded at the instigation of a woman whom King Herod loved. His father, the Prophet Zakariyya was also killed during the same period. The Quran says that peace and Allah's blessings were on Prophet Yahya, when he was born, while he lived and when he was about to die an unjust death and would continue even after his death. The name Yahya, which was chosen by Allah Himself, literally means, 'He shall live'. i.e. he shall be spiritually alive and remembered forever.

▶ **Moral**: All the prophets of Allah paved the way for the next messenger of Allah till the Prophet Muhammad, the last messenger, came.

▶ **Key Events**: The Prophet Yahya's message, his death.

▶ **See the Quran**: *Aal-Imran* 3:39; *Al-Anam* 6:85; *Maryam* 19:6-15; *Al-Anbiyaa* 21:90.

▶ **See in this book**: Hannah, Isa, Maryam and Zakariyya.

▶ **Relatives**:

Father	-	the Prophet Zakariyya
Mother	-	Isha bint Faqudh
Aunt	-	Hannah
Cousins	-	Maryam
	-	the Prophet Isa

▶ **Study Question**: What was the mission of the Prophet Yahya?

What sort of life did the Prophet Yahya live?

Yajuj and Majuj

Yajuj and Majuj (Gog and Magog) were wild tribes of central Asia who used to attack people during the reign of King Dhu'l Qarnayn. He raised an iron wall to protect his people from their invasions.

The Quran says that when the Day of Judgement was near, Yajuj and Majuj would be everywhere on the earth. This would be a sign that the Day of Judgement was approaching.

▶ **Moral**: It is Allah who provides ways and means to help and protect His people.

▶ **Key Events**: Raising of the wall.

▶ **See the Quran:** *Al-Kahf* 18:83-101; *Al- Anbiyaa* 21:96.

▶ **See in this book:** Dhu'l- Qarnayn.

▶ **Study Question**: Who were Yajuj and Majuj?

Yaqub

Yaqub (Jacob) was the son of the Prophet Ishaq (Isaac) and father of the Prophet Yusuf (Joseph) and was himself a Prophet. Allah made him truthful and righteous. He was also known as Israil, which means 'servant of Allah'. The Children of Israel tribe was named after him. Allah gave the news of his birth to his grandfather, the Prophet Ibrahim (Abraham), calling him 'a gift' (*nafila*) even before the birth of his father the Prophet Ishaq.

The Prophet Yaqub lived in Jerusalem in the 19th B.C. He had twelve sons. His most loved son, the Prophet Yusuf, was thrown into a well by his jealous stepbrothers. The Prophet Yaqub was blinded by sorrow, but he remained patient. He turned to Allah in his pain and suffering, but never complained. He knew that Allah was merciful and beneficent and he had perfect faith in Him. He never gave up hope for the Prophet Yusuf, though people called him a mad old man.

The Prophet Yusuf was saved and was taken to Egypt where he later became the most trusted minister of the Egyptian king. The Prophet Yaqub's eyesight was restored when his eyes were touched by the Prophet Yusuf's shirt. Later the Prophet Yaqub settled in Egypt with all the members of his family.

He asked his children always to worship Allah and follow the true faith even after his death. They promised to follow the true faith, the faith of the Prophets Ibrahim, Ismail and Ishaq. The Prophet Yaqub died at the age of 143 years and was buried in Hebron near Jerusalem.

▶ **Moral**: Allah is always merciful to His believers. He never disappoints them.

▶ **Key Events**: Loss of the Prophet Yusuf, reuniting with the Prophet Yusuf.

▶ **See the Quran**: *Al-Baqarah* 2:132-133; *Aal-Imran* 3:93; *Al-An'am* 6:84; *Yusuf* 12:86; *Maryam* 19:49-50; *Al-Anbiyaa* 21:72.

▶ **See in this book**: Children of Israel, Binyamin, Ibrahim, Ishaq and Yusuf.

▶ **Relatives**:

Grandfather	-	the Prophet Ibrahim
Father	-	the Prophet Ishaq
Son	-	the Prophet Yusuf
Wife	-	Rahil

▶ **Study Question**: Who was the Prophet Yaqub?

What was the nature of his suffering?

Yauq

Yauq was a pagan idol worshipped during the times of the Prophet Nuh (Noah). Yauq was in the shape of a horse representing swiftness. The other four idols worshipped at that time were: Wadd, Suwa, Yaghuth and Nasr.

▶ **Moral**: It makes no sense to worship Allah's creation but not Allah.

▶ **Key Events**: The Prophet Nuh's message, great flood.

▶ **See the Quran:** *Nuh* 71:23.

▶ **See in this book:** Nasr, Nuh, Suwaa, Wadd and Yaguth.

▶ **Study Question**: What was Yauq and what did it represent?

Yunus

In 800 B.C, the Prophet Yunus (Jonah) who belonged to the Binyamin (Benjamin) tribe, was sent to the people of Nineveh, a very ancient town near the River Tigris, opposite the city of Mosul and approximately 230 miles north-west of Baghdad. The tomb of Nabi Yunus can still be seen there.

Ninevah had been a great and glorious city, but later became a city of sin. The people of the town were wicked. The Prophet Yunus asked them to leave their old ways and follow the laws of Allah. He preached faith in Allah and in His Unity and the value of righteousness. But they did not listen to him. They did not believe that he was a messenger from Allah and made a mockery of him. This angered the Prophet Yunus. He warned them that Allah would punish them for their sins. He then left the city, discouraged at the failure of his mission.

He went to the sea coast and boarded a ship. When the ship sailed out into deep waters there was a violent storm. The sailors, thought that their ill-luck was because of the Prophet Yunus, whom they thought to be a slave. So they threw him into the sea, where he was swallowed alive by a whale. Inside the whale's body in pitch darkness he was very sad and realised his mistake. He should not have acted in anger or left his people without being ordered to do so by Allah. He should have been more patient and asked himself who he was to judge people and announce Allah's punishment. He had departed in anger, forgetting that Allah showed mercy and forgiveness. He had run away as if to escape from Allah's plan. He asked Allah to pardon him for his mistake. He sincerely repented and acknowledged Allah's goodness and mercy. Allah then forgave him. If he had not realised his mistake and asked for Allah's pardon, the Quran says that he would have stayed

inside the whale till the Day of Judgement. When he came out he felt ill, but he took refuge under the gourd tree and also ate its juicy fruits. He returned to the town and continued his mission and, in spite of all kinds of obstacles, he continued his work till the people returned to the right path. Allah's plan always prevails. One should never judge others, as only Allah can judge and decide whom to punish or to pardon.

The Prophet Yunus is also called Dhu'n-Nun and Sahib al-Hut, meaning the 'Man of a Fish'. The tenth *surah* of the Quran is also named after him.

▶ **Moral**: One should never lose hope and always seek help from Allah. Allah saves His believers miraculously. Only Allah can decide who is righteous or wicked and who should be punished or pardoned. Allah forgives if one truly repents.

▶ **Key Events**: The Prophet Yunus's giving up his mission, swallowed by whale, return to his mission, successful in his mission.

▶ **See the Quran**: *An-Nisaa* 4:163, *Al-An'am* 6:86; *Yunus* 10:93-103; *Al-Anbiyaa* 21:87-88; *As-Saffat* 37:139-148; *Al-Qalam* 68:48.

▶ **Study Question**: Why was the Prophet Yunus swallowed by the whale?

What happened when he was inside the whale?

What are the other names of the Prophet Yunus?

Yusha bin Nun

The Quran mentions Yusha bin Nun (Joshua) twice, though without naming him, as the young disciple of the Prophet Musa (Moses), who accompanied him when he went on a long journey to meet Al-Khidr.

The Prophet Musa wanted to take the Children of Israel into the holy land, but they did not want to go because they were scared to fight the giants (the Amalekites) who lived there. It was only Yusha bin Nun and Kalab (Caleb) who encouraged them to go. They pleaded for immediate entry. Yusha bin Nun and Kalab said that they must put their trust in Allah for victory and should go inside from the proper entrance. But the Children of Israel refused to enter the holy land as they were scared to fight due to their lack of faith in Allah. They wandered homeless for 40 years. Yusha bin Nun became the leader of the Children of Israel after the Prophet Musa. Later it was Yusha bin

Nun, who led the Children of Israel to fight the Amalekites, ultimately conquering Palestine and Syria and entered the holy land.

▶ **Moral**: Faith in Allah gives one strength to do anything, including the impossible.

▶ **Key Events**: War with the Amalekites and victory of the Children of Israel.

▶ **See the Quran**: *Al-Maidah* 5:23; *Al-Kahf* 18:60-63.

▶ **See in this book**: The Children of Israel, Kalab, Al-Khidr and Musa.

▶ **Study Question**: Who was Yusha bin Nun?

Why were the Children of Israel scared to enter the holy land?

How did they conquer Palestine and Syria?

Yusuf

The Prophet Muhammad called the Prophet Yusuf (Joseph) the noblest of all the prophets. He was a prophet from a long line of prophets. He was the son of the Prophet Yaqub (Jacob) whose father and grandfather were the Prophet Ishaq (Isaac) and Prophet Ibrahim (Abraham) respectively. *Surah* 12 of the Quran is named after him.

He was born in Canaan, near Nablus, some thirty miles north of Jerusalem. He was the second youngest of the twelve sons of the

Prophet Yaqub. His mother was Rahil (Rachael) who had been childless for many years. Rahil had one more son, Binyamin, (Benjamin) Yusuf's little brother. The Quran calls the Prophet Yusuf's story the 'most beautiful story' (*ahsan al-qasas*). The Prophet Yusuf's story is beautiful because it is a sign of the working of Allah's plan and purpose in man's chequered history. It is also more detailed than any other story in the Quran.

The Prophet Yusuf was righteous, true, frank and gentle, even as a child. His father loved him dearly. His stepbrothers were jealous of him and hated him. One day the Prophet Yusuf dreamt that eleven stars, the sun and the moon were prostrating themselves in front of him. His destiny was pre-figured in the dream. His father asked him not to inform his brothers about his dream because they might become even more jealous of him. The Prophet Yaqub told him that Allah would teach him to understand dreams. He had also chosen him for greater purpose.

Meanwhile, his stepbrothers planned to get rid of him so that they had no rivals for their father's love and favours. One day they took him to the forest after convincing their father that they would take good care of him. They wanted to kill him, but one of the brothers, Yahuda (Judah), objected to this plan. Instead he suggested leaving him in a dry well. When they returned home they told their father that he had been eaten up by a wolf. As a proof, they showed him the Prophet Yusuf's shirt, which they had stained with goat's blood. The Prophet Yaqub could see that there had been foul play, but was helpless

and prayed for Allah's help. Just as the righteous take disasters with humble devotion and belief in Allah's will, so also did the Prophet Yusuf. And Allah's will was to save him. After three days a caravan of Midianite or Arab merchants travelling to Egypt was passing by there and found him in the well. They later sold him to Fitfir (Potiphar) for 20 dirhams. Fitfin was an officer, with the title of Aziz, in the Egyptian court. He brought him up like his own son. According to Allah's plan, the Prophet Yusuf was brought from a small village to the most advanced city of those times, Memphis, to be educated and become wise enough to understand the ways of the world, because he had eventually to rule the country.

When he grew up, Aziz's wife, Zulaykha became attracted to him. But Allah gave him the strength to reject her advances. This resistance brought him disgrace and imprisonment in this world for a time. By an evil plan she had him put in jail. But Allah had his own plans. Allah was with the Prophet Yusuf in all his difficulties, sorrows and sufferings, as He is with all His servants who put their trust in Him. Going to prison opened another chapter in the Prophet Yusuf's life. The plan of Allah developed. The wicked might plot, but in the end everything is used as part of the Universal Plan for beneficent purposes.

The Prophet Yusuf's mission was far higher than that of merely foretelling events. He taught the truth of Allah and the Hereafter to mankind. He received his prophethood in prison and preached the unity of Allah. His listeners were Egyptians, no doubt steeped in materialism, magic and polytheism. He told them that the only reality was Allah. Authority could come from Him alone. That was the only true religion. The Prophet Yusuf told them about his heritage of great men known for their wisdom and truthfulness—the Prophets Ibrahim, Ishaq and Yaqub. It was Allah's Grace that had taught them just as Allah's Grace teaches all mankind. In the prison he interpreted the dreams of two prisoners. One of them told him of a dream in which he saw himself pressing grapes to make wine. The other one saw himself carrying some bread on his head which was pecked at by birds. To the first, he said he would soon be released from jail and would pour wine for his master. To the other, he said that he would be sentenced to death and birds would peck at his head. The Prophet Yusuf asked the one who would serve wine in the royal court to mention to the king how cruelly he had been thrown into prison, although he was completely innocent.

His prediction came true. One of his companions was released and was appointed as a cup-bearer to the king. But he forgot to mention the Prophet Yusuf to the king. The Prophet Yusuf suffered in prison for several more years.

One day, the king asked his courtiers to interpret a strange dream which he had had. He dreamt that seven weak cows were eating seven fat ones and seven green ears of corn were being replaced by seven dry ones. No one could give a suitable answer. At this point the cup-bearer was reminded of the Prophet Yusuf's ability to interpret dreams. He rushed to him in his cell and asked him about the dream. The Prophet Yusuf told him it meant that there would be seven years of abundant crops followed by seven years of dreadful famine. After that, there would be a year of abundance during which the people would press the grapes. He also advised that in the first seven years the greater

part of whatever crops were grown should be saved. The king was very pleased and called for the Prophet Yusuf. But he refused to come unless cleared of the false charges made by Zulaykha. The king ordered an enquiry into the Prophet Yusuf's complaint and found that all the charges were false. Zulaykha admitted her crime and thus the Prophet Yusuf was released from prison with honour. The king was very impressed by his extraordinary personality, especially when his innocence, wisdom, truth and trustworthiness had been proved. The king honoured him and appointed him as his most trusted minister to look after the granaries. And thus Allah established the Prophet Yusuf in a foreign land when he was just 30 years old.

His prediction came true. In the years of abundance he saved the crops and in the days of famine Egypt could even give grain to the neighbouring countries. People came to the Prophet Yusuf from far

and wide to procure grain. His stepbrothers too came to him but they could not recognise him, though the Prophet Yusuf recognised them. He asked them about their family and they told him that they had old parents and one younger brother whose name was Binyamin. The Prophet Yusuf asked them to bring him also the next time, so that he could give more grain to them. But their father refused to send Binyamin with them as he did not trust them. Later he agreed after they took a solemn oath.

While the grain for Binyamin was being weighed out, the Prophet Yusuf put his drinking cup in his younger brother's packs. It was a gesture of great effection for his younger brother. But in the meanwhile, a measuring cup belonging to the king had been misplaced, and the courtiers suspected the brothers of stealing it. When the packs were opened, there, glinting in the sun, nestled a precious cup—in Binyamin's bag! This was not the cup they were actually looking for, but it was a similar one. Thus the guards mistakenly thought that Binyamin had stolen the cup. Thus Binyamin was held in Egypt. At this point Yahuda offered to stay instead of him. The Prophet Yusuf refused. The stepbrothers felt self-righteous when Binyamin was caught. They said they were not surprised as his brother, implying the Prophet Yusuf, had also been a thief. When they returned and told their father, he became very upset and blamed them for his loss. After some time, the brothers again in great need of grain, went to the Prophet Yusuf. This time they did not have enough money to buy the grain and told him of their poor condition and of their father who had

lost his eye-sight. The Prophet Yusuf then revealed his true identity to them. The stepbrothers were ashamed of themselves. But the Prophet Yusuf was benevolent and forgave them and also asked for Allah's forgiveness for them. He gave them a shirt of his and asked them to touch his father's eyes with it as this would restore his sight. He also asked them to bring his parents to him. When their caravan reached their hometown, the Prophet Yaqub could feel the breath of the Prophet Yusuf. People mocked him as they always did when he would say that the Prophet Yusuf was alive. When the brothers put the shirt on their father's eyes, his sight was restored. The brothers then asked their father to forgive them for their sins. He said that he would ask Allah to forgive them.

When the entire family came to the Prophet Yusuf, he made his parents sit on the throne. At that time his brothers bowed to him in respect. The Prophet Yusuf reminded his father about his childhood dream, which Allah had fulfilled. He then prayed to Allah and thanked him for giving him everything and for protecting him. He also prayed that Allah's blessings would continue and vowed always to submit to the Will of Allah.

It is said that the Prophet Yusuf died at the age of 110 years, 64 years before the birth of the Prophet Musa.

▶ **Moral**: Allah's eternal purpose is fulfilled by His plan in which at all times is a marvel of perfection in its working. It is in evidence throughout all the contradiction of life and changes with only the virtue of enduring nature.

▶ **Key Events**: Leaving the Prophet Yusuf in the well, sale of the Prophet Yusuf to Aziz, the Prophet Yusuf being in jail, interpretation of the king's dream, the coming of his stepbrothers for food, his forgiveness.

▶ **See the Quran**: *Al-Anam* 6:84; *Hud* 11:34; *Yusuf* 12:1-102.

▶ **See in this book**: Aziz, Binyamin, Yahuda, Yaqub and Zulaykha.

▶ **Relatives**:

Father	-	the Prophet Yaqub
Mother	-	Rahil
Brother	-	Binyamin

▶ **Study Question**: Why did the Prophet Yusuf's brothers leave him in the well?

Who rescued him out of the well and what did they do with him?

Why was the Prophet Yusuf imprisoned?

Where did he get receive his prophethood?

How did he get out of prison?

What was the king's dream?

How was the Prophet Yusuf reunited with his family?

How does the Prophet Yusuf's story show the working of Allah's plan and its purpose?

Zakariyya

Zakariyya, himself a prophet was the father of the Prophet Yahya (John the Baptist). He was an uncle of Maryam (Mary) and the priest of a temple in Jerusalem. The Prophet Zakariyya (Zacharias) was made Maryam's guardian when she was dedicated to the service of Allah.

In his old age he prayed to Allah for a son. He did not want a son merely to continue his family, but to carry forward the work of Allah sincerely, for his people were not good followers of Allah. An angel then came and told him about the birth of the Prophet Yahya. He wondered how this could be possible, when he was old and his wife was barren. The angel said whatever Allah willed, it happened. Allah cured his wife of barrenness and raised her spiritual dignity by making her the mother of the Prophet Yahya. As a sign the angel asked him

not to speak to anyone for three days and to celebrate by praising Allah and glorifying Him in the morning and in the evening. Allah blessed him with a son who was noble, chaste and a prophet. All three of them were worthy of each other. The Quran expresses admiration for Zakariyya and his family.

▶ **Moral**: Everything is possible for Allah. Allah helps believers in wonderful ways. He always hears the prayers of His servants.

▶ **Key Events**: Birth of the Prophet Yahya, killing of the Prophet Yahya.

▶ **See the Quran**: *Aal-Imran* 3:37-42; *Al-Anam* 6:85; *Maryam* 19:2-15; *Al-Anbiyya* 21:89-90.

▶ **See in this book**: Hannah, Isa, Maryam and Yahya.

▶ **Relatives**:

Son	-	the Prophet Yahya
Wife	-	Isha bint Faqudh
Cousins	-	Hannah, Maryam, the Prophet Isa

▶ **Study Question**: Why did the Prophet Zakariyya want a son?

Zayd ibn Haritha

Zayd ibn Haritha was one of the first converts to Islam. Zayd was a slave who was given to the Prophet Muhammad by his wife Khadijah. After a few years, when his family came to take him back, he refused to go and begged to stay with the Prophet Muhammad. In return the

Prophet gave him his freedom and Zayd became his adopted son. At that time he was even called Zayd ibn Muhammad. But Surah *Al-Ahzab* 33.5 of the Quran prohibited changing the true identity of adopted sons as was the pagan custom. Adopted sons are not equal to natural sons. Thereafter Zayd was once again called by his actual father's name. To give Zayd respect in society and to remove the pre-Islamic custom in Arabia of looking down upon slaves even after they had been set free, the Prophet arranged for him to be married to his cousin, Zaynab bint Jahsh. But the marriage did not turn out to be happy. She was rich and high-born and looked down upon Zayd. Both were good and loved the Prophet Muhammad, but as individuals, they were very different and therefore incompatible. Zayd wanted to divorce Zaynab but the Prophet asked him to give more time to it.

When a marriage is unhappy, Islam permits the bond to be dissolved, provided that the interests of all concerned are safeguarded. Finally, they had a divorce. After Zaynab had completed the period of waiting (*iddah*), the Prophet Muhammad himself married her at the behest of Allah. This marriage put an end to the pre-Islamic pagan custom which considered an adopted son equal to a natural son.

Later Zayd was killed by the Byzantines in the village of Mu'ta near the Dead Sea in what is now called Jordan.

▶ **Moral**: Man-made relationships cannot be equal to blood relationships. Truth cannot be changed by man-made laws.

▶ **Key Events**: Zayd obtaining his freedom, becoming the adopted son of the Prophet, marriage to and later divorce from Zaynab bint Jahsh.

▶ **See the Quran**: *Al-Ahzab* 33:5, 37, 38.

▶ **See in this book**: Zaynab bint Jahsh.

▶ **Relationship**:

Foster father	-	the Prophet Muhammad
Wife	-	Zaynab

▶ **Study Question**:

Who was Zayd ibn Haritha?

Why did the Prophet have Zayd married to Zaynab?

Why did Zaynab and Zayd have a divorce?

What does Islam say about marriage?

Which pagan custom was put to an end by the marriage of the Prophet Muhammad to Zaynab bint Jahsh?

Zaynab bint Jahsh

Zaynab bint Jahsh was a cousin of the Prophet Muhammad and belonged to a rich family. The Prophet Muhammad had her married to Zayd ibn Haritha. But this marriage did not last long due to the basic differences between them. Allah does not want marriage to be a

bond which tortures people but a source of happiness. Eventually Zaynab and Zayd had a divorce.

Then the Prophet Muhammad himself married Zaynab. The Prophet Muhammad's marriage to Zaynab, a divorced wife of his adopted son, Zayd, put an end to the pre-Islamic custom according to which an adopted son was considered equal to a natural son. Islam does not allow a father to marry his natural son's divorced wife.

The adoptive relationship was not a blood tie and was therefore no bar to marriage. With marriage to Prophet Muhammad, Zaynab obtained the dearest wish of her heart, i.e. being raised to the status of 'Mother of the Believers' with all the dignity and responsibility of the position. She worked for the poor, providing for them out of the earnings of her manual work, as she was skilled in leather craft.

- ▶ **Moral**: Marriages are made on earth, not in heaven. When marriage is unhappy it is better to be dissolved.

- ▶ **Key Events**: Divorce from Zayd ibn Haritha, marriage to the Prophet Muhammad.

- ▶ **See the Quran**: *Al-Ahzab* 33:28, 50.

- ▶ **See in this book:** Muhammad, Ummahat al-Muminin and Zayd ibn Haritha.

- ▶ **Relatives**: Husband - the Prophet Muhammad

- ▶ **Study Question**: What was the dearest wish of Zaynab bint Jahsh?

Zulaykha

Zulaykha was the wife of Fitfir (Potiphar) who is called Aziz in the Quran. He was a high-ranking officer at the Egyptian court. Without naming her, the Quran describes her at length as the one who attempted to seduce the Prophet Yusuf (Joseph).

Aziz had bought the Prophet Yusuf as a slave for 20 dirhams. But he treated the Prophet Yusuf with honour and like a son rather than as a slave. The Prophet Yusuf grew up to be a good-looking man. Aziz's wife, Zulaykha, was madly attracted to him. One day when her husband was out, she called the Prophet Yusuf into her room and bolted the doors. She tried to attract him to earthly pleasure and to commit a

sin. He begged her not to force him into sin. He told her that her love was sinful and they had to be honest to her husband. But she was blind with her passion and his requests had no influence on her. His faith in Allah made him stronger and he knew that Allah was watching them. When he rushed to the door, she tore his shirt from the back in order to stop him. When Aziz arrived and saw this, she put the blame on the Prophet Yusuf and asked her husband to punish him. But the Prophet Yusuf denied the charges. Then a wise man of the family said if the Prophet Yusuf's shirt was torn from the front she was right, but if from the back then he was right. So the Prophet Yusuf was saved. Aziz even asked Zulaykha to seek his forgiveness. The news of this incident spread throughout the town, particularly among the women, and they started making fun of Zulaykha.

To justify her deed, she invited all the noble ladies to her house.

She gave each of them a knife and asked them to cut fruit with it. At that time she asked the Prophet Yusuf to pass through the dining room. The ladies were so struck by his beauty that they lost their self-control and cut their fingers instead. In this way Zulaykha tried to justify her act and win the support of society.

Zulaykha continued to trouble the Prophet Yusuf and threatened to have him imprisoned. He knew human weakness and prayed to Allah not to let him commit this sin. He cried out for Allah's help and said that prison would be better than sinning. But due to her evil plans, he was imprisoned for many years. Later, when the king set up an enquiry to find out whether the Prophet Yusuf was guilty, Zulaykha confessed her sin freely and frankly. Finally, the ProphetYusuf's innocence was proved.

▶ **Moral:** The credit for our being saved from sin must go to Allah. We can only try to be true and sincere and seek Allah's help. Allah will purify us and save us from all that is wrong.

▶ **Key Events:** Coming of the Prophet Yusuf, the Prophet Yusuf's rejection of Zulaykha's advances.

▶ **See the Quran:** *Yusuf* 12.

▶ **See in this book:** Aziz and Yusuf.

▶ **Relatives:** Husband - Fitfir

▶ **Study Question:** What was the sin of Zulaykha?

Why did she invite the noble ladies to her house?